FIGHTING TO KEEP MY JOB

CASE STUDY OF A UNITED NATIONS RETIREE

WRITTEN BY

PETER E. TEMU

Bloomington, IN  Milton Keynes, UK

authorHOUSE®

AuthorHouse™
1663 Liberty Drive, Suite 200
Bloomington, IN 47403
www.authorhouse.com
Phone: 1-800-839-8640

AuthorHouse™ UK Ltd.
500 Avebury Boulevard
Central Milton Keynes, MK9 2BE
www.authorhouse.co.uk
Phone: 08001974150

This book is a work of non-fiction. Unless otherwise noted, the author and the publisher make no explicit guarantees as to the accuracy of the information contained in this book and in some cases, names of people and places have been altered to protect their privacy.

First published by AuthorHouse 4/9/2007

ISBN: 978-1-4343-0009-6 (e)
ISBN: 978-1-4343-0008-9 (sc)

Library of Congress Control Number: 2007901555

Printed in the United States of America
Bloomington, Indiana

This book is printed on acid-free paper.

THIS BOOK IS DEDICATED
TO MEMBERS OF MY FAMILY.

To my wife, Irene, and my children
Dorothy, Caroline, Angela,
Benjamin, Edwin, and Flavia.

Acknowledgements.

I owe a debt of gratitude to my family, to whom I have dedicated this book. In particular, when the going was rough, my wife, Irene, was always there for me. I thank her sincerely for her perseverance and understanding, and for giving me the warmth, comfort, and solace which I needed to keep my spirits high, as the fight for my job intensified.

Our six children, all of whom, at the time, were either at school or college in the United States of America, were already mature enough to understand how the loss of my job would have affected their young lives. One of them, Angela, seeing that I was writing a book on the subject, kept saying, impatiently, "Dad, I can't wait to read the book".

A special word of thanks goes to my son-in-law, Mr. Shadrack Ngowi, without whose help and excellent computer skills, I would not have been able to deliver the manuscript in time for publication.

Contents

LIST OF ACRONYMS.

ACC	Administrative Committee on Co-ordination
ASG	Assistant Secretary-General (of the United Nations)
DEVPLAN	Ministry of Economic Affairs and Development Planning (Tanzania)
DIESA	Department of International Economic and Social Affairs
ESAMI	Eastern and Southern African Management Institute
ERCA	External Relations and Council Affairs (section of WFC)
ECOSOC	Economic and Social Council (of the United Nations)
ECA	Economic Commission for Africa (of the United Nations)
FAO	Food and Agriculture Organization of the United Nations
IDE	Institute of Developing Economies (Tokyo, Japan)
IDS	Institute for Development Studies (Nairobi, Kenya)
IFM	Institute of Finance Management (Dar es Salaam, Tanzania)
IFPRI	International Food Policy Research Institute (Washington, DC)

IMF	International Monetary Fund
JAB	Joint Appeals Board (of the United Nations)
MULPOC	Multinational Programming and Operational Centre (ECA)
OAU	Organization for African Unity
OHRM	Office of Human Resources Management (of the United Nations)
PDEA	Policy Development and Economic Analysis (section of WFC)
PER	Performance Evaluation Report
SADCC	Southern African Development Co-ordination Conference
TCDC	Technical Co-operation among Developing Countries
UN	United Nations
UNDP	United Nations Development Programme
UNIDO	United Nations Industrial Development Organization
UNPAAERD	United Nations Programme of Action for African Recovery and Development
USAID	United States Agency for International Development
USG	Under-Secretary-General (of the United Nations)
WFC	World Food Council (of the United Nations)
WFP	World Food Programme (of the United Nations)

INTRODUCTION AND SUMMARY

This book is, in part, an autobiography - but only in part, because I did not feel that a full story of my life would be of particular interest to the reader. I did feel, however, that specific aspects of my life story would be of interest to the general reader, and would particularly attract the type of reader whose experience bears some resemblance to mine.

In addition, I believe that the experiences recounted in this book will be an object lesson to all those involved in administration and personnel management - particularly as concerns recruitment, retrenchment, and on-job performance evaluation – because they are a reminder of the rigorous standards of professional integrity and fair play that these exercises invariably call for.

The book is about my employment history: first, in my own country, Tanzania, and later at the United Nations. It covers my entire working life, from the time I graduated as a student from Makerere College, in Uganda, in 1962, to my retirement from the United Nations service in 1996. Quite intentionally, the book says nothing about my life prior to 1962, or after my retirement in 1996, or outside the scope of my employment experience.

The focus of the narrative is on the relation between me and my immediate boss at the workplace. In 1976, while employed as

National Planning Controller in the Ministry of Finance and Planning in Tanzania, my boss, the Principal Secretary, tried to get rid of me, for reasons of his own. I fought against the decision, and won. Years later, in 1989, while employed as Chief of the United Nations World Food Council Liaison Office in New York, my boss, the Executive Director, tried to get rid of me, also for reasons of his own. After a protracted fight, I won, and retained my job. Had I lost the fight in either of these two cases, it would probably have spelt a disastrous end to my working career.

The book says little, in any detail, about my 1976 episode at the Ministry in Tanzania, largely because the experience is undocumented. At that time, little was done by way of correspondence. Decisions at any level were just made politically, by those in power, and instructions handed down verbally to their subordinates. The whole matter, crucial as it was to me, was over – and thank God, in my favour - within days.

Not so with the 1989 episode in New York. This one degenerated into one long-drawn three-year struggle. It was carried on at the legal and non-legal levels; entailed political and professional lobbying; and was waged now openly, now clandestinely, as circumstances dictated. The struggle was ruthless and relentless; and it is memories of it that have prompted me to write this book.

Sparked off by a letter from my boss dated 12 June 1989, in which the Executive Director of the World Food Council said that I should quit my job by 31 December 1989, this particular struggle went through four distinct phases. The first phase lasted from June 1989 to June1990. During this period I made every effort to have the dispute resolved amicably. I pleaded and tried to negotiate with the Executive Director, Mr. Gerald Trant, and with the Assistant Secretary-General for Human Resources Management, Mr. Kofi Annan, but all in vain. Any appearances of reconciliation turned out to be purely illusory.

The second phase began with my formal launching in July 1990 of an appeal to the United Nations Joint Appeals Board against the Executive Director's decision to have me dismissed from the Council. It ended in April 1991 with the conclusion of the legal process, whereby the Joint Appeals Board found fault with the Administration, and ruled in my favour, causing the Secretary-General of the United Nations to instruct the Executive Director to restore me to my original position.

The third phase of the struggle lasted from April to November 1991. During this period, the Executive Director tried in vain to dodge the implementation of the Secretary-General's directive, and relied on procrastination and all forms of delaying tactics to stall the process. It was not until November 1991 - a full seven months after he had been ordered to do so - that the Executive Director finally yielded, and invited me to take up my position in Rome.

The fourth phase of the fight began with my return to Rome in November 1991, and ended with the Executive Director's final exit from the Council in December 1992. During the whole of this period (except at the very start, when I had an open clash with him) the fight was largely subterranean, but there was no mistaking its presence. Its root cause lay in his announcement that he did not consider me "a perfect match" for the responsibilities he had assigned me in Rome. Naturally, I took his statement to mean that he had accepted me against his will. I considered it offensive for him to have stated it publicly, and I said so. That is exactly what caused my initial clash with him, and why I was on constant alert ever after, in case the Executive Director tried to sabotage my work.

The entire record of the conflict between the Executive Director and I is fully documented, and the relevant correspondence, which I carefully preserved, is reproduced verbatim in the Annex to the book. In fact, a reading of the Annex alone is sufficient to give the reader both the substance and the flavour of the entire history.

Nothing in the book is based on rumours or hearsay. As a historical account, the narrative is true and accurate, and contains neither unwarranted criticism, nor undue fear, of those prominent figures within the United Nations in whose hands my future lay. These figures were, in order of seniority: the Under-Secretary-General, Mr. Martti Ahtisaari, who later became President of Finland; Mr. Richard Foran, who succeeded Mr. Ahtisaari as Under-Secretary-General; the Assistant Secretary-General, Office of Human Resources and Management, Mr. Kofi Annan, who later served for ten years as U.N. Secretary-General; and the Executive Director of the World Food Council, Mr. Gerald Trant (now deceased). Between them, these four top bosses held my future in their hands. Faithfully recounted in the text are my dealings with them, at every step of the way, as my job crisis worsened and was then resolved.

This record has been preserved – and the entire book written – with a view to presenting an undistorted picture of the unfortunate events that took place. On a wider front, the record may also be viewed as containing important lessons for workers and their bosses, whether in or outside the United Nations.

If the book has any moral, it lies in its implicit message to executive heads and to human resources managers, charged with the task of retrenching workers: they need to go about their sensitive task conscientiously and with integrity, avoiding favouritism, and playing strictly by the rules. They must resist the temptation to use their privileged position to settle scores by victimising colleagues against whom they may bear personal grudges. The message is equally pertinent for teachers at civil service training institutions, and schools of management and administration, as an elementary lesson in professional ethics to be taught to students. All these will find the book well worth reading.

The Executive Director of the World Food Council (like the Principal Secretary of the Ministry of Finance and Planning, in Tanzania, before him) failed the test of honesty and impartiality when they tried to get rid of me for no just cause. The result was not only the permanent and totally unnecessary animosity between us but, more tragically, as one of our colleagues put it, "the lack of collegiality and an abundance of professional mistrust" that grew and flourished among the senior staff of the World Food Council secretariat.

It is not by accident that during Mr. Trant's six years as Executive Director, from 1986 to 1992, the image of the Council, shaky before, progressively deteriorated, to the point that at the time of his departure, the Secretary-General of the United Nations saw no point in appointing a successor. The Council's secretariat disintegrated amidst all forms of internal recrimination, and no other ministerial session was ever convened until the United Nations World Food Council finally wound up unceremoniously in 1996.

PART ONE
BEFORE JOINING THE UNITED NATIONS

CHAPTER I

1961, 1962

THE BACKGROUND: ERA OF INDEPENDENCE.

"Young Tanzanians who graduated then never looked for jobs.
Jobs looked for them"

If there was ever a time in my life to which the proverbial 'good old days' could plausibly be applied, the early 1960s was it. At that time, one felt good to be an African, and good to be a Tanzanian; one felt good to be young, and good to be a university graduate.

"The wind of change is sweeping all over Africa", Harold Macmillan said, in a speech delivered in Cape Town, South Africa. Here was a British Prime Minister, the leading colonial power, publicly acknowledging the 'wind' of political change. Imagine how much more we, the young Africans of the day, must have sensed it!

The struggle for freedom was on in earnest. Colonialism was on the run, fighting a losing battle. Everywhere, independence was in the air.   .

During this time – on December 9, 1961, to be exact – my country, Tanzania, attained its independence from Britain. And, barely five months later, in April 1962, at 25 years of age, I graduated from Makerere University College in Uganda with a BSc(Economics)(Honours), an external degree of the University of London.

Young Tanzanians who graduated then never looked for jobs. Jobs looked for them. Under the policy of 'Africanization', jobs were literally up for grabs. Any young Tanzanian with secondary school education or better, was virtually assured of an office job, and anyone holding a university degree was simply hot cake!

In these circumstances, it is little wonder that prospective employers, including government ministries, would identify eligible university students long before their final year, offering them temporary jobs during their annual vacations as an inducement to join them after their graduation. In my particular case, during the three years – 1959, 1960 and 1961 – preceding my graduation, I accepted temporary jobs, in turn, from three different employers: the Tanganyika Planting Company, which was a Danish private sugar company; the Lint and Seed Marketing Board, a public parastatal organization; and the Government Ministry of Finance.

When I graduated in 1962, I could easily have taken up employment with any one of them, had I so wished. In the event, I chose none of them. Instead, I decided to take up a teaching job as economics tutor in the Department of Extra-Mural Studies at the University College, Dar es Salaam, in Tanganyika (later renamed Tanzania).

CHAPTER II

1962 TO 1970
EMPLOYMENT IN ACADEMIA:
TANZANIA AND KENYA.

*"I realized that while my country regarded me as a
highly educated man, the wider world did not"*

Soon after my graduation, I was posted to the University College, Dar es Salaam, to be Organizing Tutor in the same Extra-Mural department. Only recently established, the whole of the University College, Dar es Salaam occupied a single one-storey building at Lumumba Street in the City of Dar es Salaam. It had only three faculties: - Law; Public Administration; and Extra-Mural Studies. Charged with organising adult education classes in Dar es Salaam, Morogoro and Tanga Regions, the Department of Extra-Mural Studies had only two academic staff members, including myself. My supervisor, Dr. Allan Slee, himself reported to the Director of Extra-Mural Studies, at Makerere College, Kampala, Uganda.

At the end of 1962, I left Dar es Salaam to take up the post of Economics Tutor at the College of Social Studies, a residential adult education college, located at Kikuyu, Kenya, some 12 miles from the capital city of Nairobi. Originally under the auspices of the Makerere Extra-Mural Department, this small college was soon to be integrated into the University of Nairobi to become the Department of Residential Adult Education. Since the three university campuses – Makerere, Dar es Salaam and Nairobi – were regarded as constituent colleges of a prospective University of East Africa, my transfers between them were seen as a purely internal movement, a process that was building up – rather than detracting from – my academic career.

Around mid-1965 came my next move, this time out of the College of Social Studies at Kikuyu to the Institute for Development Studies (IDS) at the University of Nairobi main campus in Nairobi city, a move that took me out of teaching into doing research. It happened that a major study on food marketing in Africa, funded by the United States Agency for International Development (USAID), had just been launched. It was a joint study involving three American universities in collaboration with three African universities. The University of Nairobi was one of the African universities chosen for the study, and I was the staff member selected to work on it.

The study was directed by Professor William O. Jones, Director of the Food Research Institute of Stanford University. My American counterpart was Professor Vance Q. Alvis of West Virginia University whose office, like mine, was located at the IDS in the University of Nairobi's main building, from where we both operated during the entire period of the study, from mid 1965 to mid 1967.

I had never done field research before. It was fascinating for Alvis and myself to be travelling from city to city, and from district to district, throughout Kenya, interviewing market agents and food traders at every level of the distribution chain.

In 1966, I attended a seminar at Stanford University where the whole research team comprising the academic staff of the six collaborating universities, led by the Stanford Food Research Institute, met to review

6

progress. Personally, I enjoyed every moment of it, not least because it was my first visit to the United States.

"Wow," said a girl I met on the Stanford campus, "You speak with a British accent! Are you from Jamaica?"

Back in Nairobi, we continued our work in the normal way. All seemed well except, perhaps, for a certain uneasiness that I began to feel as time went on. It stemmed from my growing awareness that while my American colleagues valued my contribution, none of them seemed to regard me as a really qualified academic. Though they did not say it in so many words, the message was unmistakable: I was a potentially good graduate school student, that was all.

At first, the thought of this slightly offended me. Was this the American superiority complex that I had heard so much about, or was there something more to it? The answer was not far to seek. It soon dawned on me that in America it was standard practice for university academics – assistant professors, associate professors or full professors – to have a doctorate as their *minimum* academic qualification. In my case, I had only a bachelor's degree, or an undergraduate diploma, as they would call it. I had yet to go to graduate school for my Master's and Doctoral degrees before I could count as a properly qualified academic in American eyes.

For the first time, I had a strong urge to go to graduate school. I realized that while my own country regarded me as well educated individual, the wider world did not. The fact that I was now thirty, married, with three children, did not seem to deter me. It is not surprising, therefore, that when, at the end of my research assignment at the IDS, Professor Jones invited me to apply for admission to graduate school at Stanford University, I welcomed the opportunity with open arms.

It was summer 1967, and fortune truly smiled on me. My admission to the Food Research Institute of Stanford University was granted. Moreover, I was awarded a Rockefeller Foundation fellowship under a staff development programme for East African universities. The fellowship covered all my training and living expenses in the United States for my entire family, while my home university would guarantee me a job and re-absorb me on its academic staff on my return. What more could one ask?

1967 to 1970

The stage was set. In the Fall of 1967 I commenced my graduate studies at the Food Research Institute in Stanford University, California, obtained a Master's degree by the end of 1968, and successfully completed the course work for the Doctoral programme in 1970. Before the doctorate would be awarded, however, I needed to return to Africa to do field research, write up a dissertation, and then go back to Stanford University to defend it.

That is exactly what I did. In September 1970, I returned to Tanzania, and was appointed Senior Research Fellow in the Economic Research Bureau of the University of Dar es Salaam. During that time, I carried out the necessary field research and wrote a dissertation on *Marketing Board Pricing and Storage Policy with Particular Reference to Maize in Tanzania*. My doctoral thesis was successfully defended at Stanford University, and I was awarded the PhD in 1974.

One might have thought that this award would have clinched, boosted and confirmed me on my career path as an academic. Not so. On my return to Tanzania in 1970, a most curious and unexpected twist of events occurred which placed me, willy-nilly, on a career path for the United Nations. Who could have guessed that three years after receiving my doctorate, I would be joining the international civil service, and remain there for nearly twenty years, until my retirement in 1996 ?

Chapter III

1970 to 1977
Back in Dar es Salaam, Tanzania

The period 1970 to 1977 was for me a bumpy ride on a journey that had no clearly defined destination. By 1973 I had quite happily settled down as the new Director of the Economic Research Bureau at the University of Dar es Salaam, and was looking forward to a solid academic career.

But one day there was a knock on my door, and in walked *one* Mr. Ngambikomsu Mamuya, Permanent Secretary to the Ministry of Development Planning and Economic Affairs (DEVPLAN). He had come to invite me to join DEVPLAN to fill a newly created post of National Planning Controller.

I knew my country well enough to understand that the so-called 'invitation', coming as it did from the Government and conveyed personally by DEVPLAN's top boss, was tantamount to a directive. It came at a time when the entire governmental machinery was going through a restructuring process, popularly known as 'decentralisation' in line with the recommendations of the MacKinsey Report produced by an American consultancy firm hired recently by the government. The decentralization was an all-pervasive public exercise, entailing

11

the redrawing of organizational charts at every level, from central ministries to regional, district, and even local administrations.

In the name of 'nation building' – a popular slogan at the time - the executive heads of the different public entities had been given a blank cheque: they could hire or re-deploy any Tanzanian citizen they considered suitable for a particular post in the new structure, and it was tacitly seen as unpatriotic for anyone so appointed to decline the offer. As one of the few qualified economists in the country at the time, I had already declined an earlier offer to serve as an economist in a restructured Ministry of Commerce and Industry. I knew I could not turn down one more offer, and get away with it.

Fortunately for me, this latest offer was not without its attractions. It was both prestigious and of professional interest. I was to be in charge of national planning, reporting directly to the Permanent Secretary. The Commissioner for Sectoral Planning and the Commissioner for Macro-economic Planning, each of whom headed a major planning division, were both to report to me as National Planning Controller, the central co-ordinator. Moreover, I was assured that my assignment was only for the preparatory phase of the Five-Year Development Plan, after which I would be free to resume my academic career at the University. I decided to view it all in a positive light: here was an historic opportunity for me to make a national contribution that I could look back on with pride in later years.

There was just one snag, and I was quick to point it out. Once I entered the government I would be so bogged down with day to day activities that there was a distinct risk of my forgetting to complete the PhD, and therefore ruining my future academic prospects.

Mr Mamuya eventually turned to me and asked; "Now, Mr Temu, what do you think? The government wants a quick answer, because the position must be filled right away".

"I feel greatly honoured", I said, "and I thank the government for the confidence it has shown in me by entrusting me with such high responsibilities. I am ready to take up the post right now. But please do me one favour: promise me that you will grant me at least three months leave to return to Stanford and present my doctoral dissertation."

He muttered something to the effect that a doctoral degree shouldn't really mean all that much to a Tanzanian in public service. But when I insisted that it would make all the difference to my academic career, Mr Mamuya shrugged his shoulders and said, reluctantly, 'OK. You will be given three months off when you need it'.

The following week I reported for duty at the Ministry of Economic Affairs and Development Planning. I little realized that I had thereby bade a permanent farewell to the university, ending my dream as a future academic once and for all.

For nearly a year, all was well and good. My work at the ministry proceeded smoothly. Then came September 1974, and my request to go to Stanford to present my dissertation was promptly granted – no questions asked. As had been anticipated, I was back in Dar es Salaam within three months, which is the length it had taken to clinch my PhD. But I arrived back in Dar es Salaam to find that the government had decided to abolish DEVPLAN as a separate ministry, and to merge it with the Treasury to form a new Ministry of Finance and Planning.

With no prior warning whatsoever, I was told on arrival to assume new responsibilities as Director of the Institute of Finance Management

(IFM), a high-level autonomous training institution, under the Ministry of Finance and Planning, running advanced diploma courses in banking, accountancy. auditing, financial management, and tax administration. This was another Presidential appointment, and I dutifully accepted it. As Director, I was to be both the administrative and the academic head of the institute.

The status of the institute, and the duties, benefits and privileges attached to the position of Director, were well above those of a Professor or Dean at the University of Dar es Salaam. For example, I had a diplomatic passport and was entitled to first class travel by air every time I went on mission abroad. I was also entitled to an official car and driver, who not only drove me back and forth from home to office, but also drove my children to their primary school in the morning and back home in the afternoon. Little wonder, perhaps, that my interest in returning to university academics began to wane, even as the government had begun to assign me one post after another.

Given the choice, I could have continued happily in my new job for years to come, giving of my best. But the ride continued to be bumpy, the destination uncertain. For, barely a year after my appointment as Director of the IFM, I was transferred back to the new Ministry of Finance and Planning and told to take charge, as before, of the planning wing, resuming my old title of National Planning Controller. This time I found it a bitter pill to swallow. But, once again, I dutifully obliged.

But the real test was yet to come. When it did, I threw caution to the winds, and said to myself that enough was enough. It happened that one afternoon, as I was paging through the usual pile of office papers at the Ministry, there was a knock on the door, and in walked

Mr William Butiku, the Personal Secretary to the President, and the highest ranking official in the State House.

After we had exchanged a few courtesies, Mr Butiku went straight to the point. "May I congratulate you, Dr Temu", he began. "President Nyerere has just appointed you Secretary to the Economic Committee of the Party. You will be based in Dodoma, our new capital city, and your immediate boss will be the Prime Minister, Mr Rashidi Kawawa, the Committee's Chairman. Your rank will be on a par with that of a permanent secretary in a government ministry, but your Party post will have far greater political clout. We are convinced that you are the man for the job. We wanted to announce it on the radio this evening, but due to the political nature of the assignment we thought it better to inform you first in order to be absolutely sure of your unreserved commitment."

My heart was pounding. I knew I did not want the job, but how was I to say it?.

"Mr Butiku," I said at last, "I feel greatly honoured that President Nyerere has once again shown such high confidence in me. And I am grateful to you personally for sounding me in advance. I have never before declined any presidential appointment, but this time I'm afraid I have to. I really have no choice. Just think of it: in the past four years I have held as many jobs. I am beginning to lose track of my career. If I am so good at each one of these assignments, why can't I be left alone to do the job? These repeated transfers are ruining me!."

I do not recall ever speaking so plainly before to anyone in high office. For, after taking a deep breath, I had simply said to myself, "Forget being diplomatic. I'll tell it as it is."

I could see that Mr Butiku, who had never met me before, was listening intently, even sympathetically. He was moved by what I said, but he made no comment. He simply nodded, shook my hand, and left. As we parted, I said to him that I would be putting my case in writing to avoid any possible misrepresentation, to which he readily agreed.

Back home, I sat at my desk that evening drafting a long letter, stating my case – politely but firmly – as best I knew how. "No fear, and no being diplomatic. Tell it as it is", I kept saying to myself.

Early next morning my wife delivered my letter to Mr Butiku at State House, after seeing me off at Dar es Salaam International Airport on a flight to New Delhi. I was leading a high-level delegation of public officials to India to prepare an agenda for a ministerial meeting of the Joint India-Tanzania Commission.

I returned from India a week later to find that there had been a complete overhaul at the top echelon of the Ministry of Finance and Planning. It had all happened so quickly. The two top officials – that is, the Permanent Secretary, and myself, the National Planning Controller – had been removed. The former was transferred back to the university to teach economics, while I was sent back to the IFM to resume my previous post as Director of the institute. My former deputy at the IFM, Dr Immanuel Bavu, who had been Acting Director since my departure and was apparently being groomed to take over the directorship, was also removed from his post and sent to the University of Dar es Salaam to teach sociology.

As I resumed my post at the IFM – a position I loved – I couldn't help but reflect on what I had been through in the recent past. Suddenly, everything was now as clear as daylight. Apparently, my letter to Mr Butiku had triggered it all. During my two weeks absence in India, State House had put the puzzle together: they had fathomed out just how come I had been made to change jobs four times in four years.

They had discovered that the 'advice' from the Permanent Secretary on which they had relied for their decisions had been vindictive.

State House must have concluded that my Permanent Secretary had an axe to grind, and had been using his official position to settle personal scores with me. In the first place, it had suited him to pull me out of IFM to work immediately under him at the ministry. And now it suited him to be rid of me altogether by having me sent to Dodoma to fill an obscure political post that he knew would spell my professional doom. And all this was being done in the name of the President The 'reasons' for all his recommendations were soon exposed for what they really were: malicious fabrication. Once this became clear, State House reaction was swift and ruthless. By a stroke of the pen, they remove him from his position in the Ministry, posted him back to the University of Dar es Salaam, while restoring me to my former position as Director of the IFM, with all its entitlements, benefits and privileges.

From this experience, I learned one unforgettable lesson: that in everyday life, and especially in job situations, it pays to resist – and even fight – any injustice perpetrated by your employer or immediate boss. It does not pay to shy away. I was hardly forty years old when all this happened to me in my own country, done by my own countryman, whose injustice I resisted. But a similar, if more vicious, episode (narrated later) was to confront me some fifteen years later, at the United Nations in New York, with even more glaring injustice. Applying the same lesson, I responded similarly. The fight lasted a full two years. Looking back, I am glad I mounted the fight. If I had not, I would have been trodden underfoot, instead of being the happy pensioner that I am today.

PART TWO
AFTER JOINING THE UNITED NATIONS

CHAPTER IV

1977 TO 1983
AT THE UNITED NATIONS ECONOMIC COMMISSION FOR AFRICA, ADDIS ABABA, ETHIOPIA

" ... I realized that I was a small cog in a huge global wheel which revolved around New York city in the United States of America"

To all intents and purposes, I would have been contented spending the rest of my working life as Director of the IFM. The position seemed to offer me all I needed, both by way of rewards and challenges. But fate had something else in store for me – a career with the United Nations.

It was mid-1977, and I was seated comfortably in my office at the IFM, reviewing the contents of the new course on tax administration. The phone rang. The Director of the Africa Desk in the Ministry of Foreign Affairs, Mr. Mwasakafyuka, was on the line.

"Dr. Temu", he said, "I have just received a cable from Mr. Paul Rupia, our Ambassador to Ethiopia, offering you a job at the United Nations Economic Commission for Africa at its headquarters in Addis Ababa... Would you mind dropping in at my office at 10 o'clock tomorrow so we can discuss it? If the time doesn't suit you, please suggest an alternative".

The time suited me fine, and I reported promptly. The Director showed me the cable he had received, and I read its entire contents. *Position*: Senior Economic Affairs Officer. *Level*: P-5 Step 1. *Salary*: US$ 38,190. This was more than five times my present salary. Clearly, the offer was irresistible. But I tried not to show it.

"Dr Temu, "what do we say to ECA? 'Yes' or 'No'?" The Director seemed indifferent, but I could sense that he somewhat envied me.

I replied that I liked the job, alright, but I was holding a very responsible Presidential appointment, and I had no intention of leaving it. I would have to have the green light from the government before I could accept the offer. I asked him if the Ministry of Foreign Affairs would seek the clearance for me, since doing it myself might create the impression that I was dissatisfied with my current post.

The Director saw my point. Like me, he knew our country's nationalist sentiments well enough to understand that the authorities would not take kindly to anyone in my position who appeared to be shopping around for more lucrative jobs in foreign countries. He also knew that no one was going to believe that such an attractive job offer had just come my way —as in fact it did — unsolicited.

Promising me his full cooperation, the Director said he expected to let me know within a couple of weeks exactly what the government's position was.

Two weeks came and went without a word from the Director. Much as I was eager for a response, I deliberately refrained from asking questions, as if the matter was not of much interest to me. In fact, I secretly yearned for the job, but I did not like show it too openly.

Imagine my delight then when, two days later, a messenger walked into my office and handed me a letter from the Minister of Finance and Planning, confirming that the President had agreed that I take up the United Nations post on secondment for two years. For the entire period of my secondment, I would be regarded as being on *leave without pay*. However, the Minister wanted me to remain at the IFM and preside over the next graduation ceremony scheduled for September. That is exactly what I did. Once my students had received their diploma certificates, I boarded a plane for Addis Ababa on 24 September 1977, which is the day I officially reported for duty in the United Nations.

Who would have thought that the day I landed in Addis Ababa, was to mark the beginning of a life-long career with the United Nations, a career which was to last nearly 20 years, and which would move me from one duty station to another: from Addis Ababa to Rome; Rome to New York; back to Rome again; and finally from Rome to Lusaka, from where I would retire at the end of February 1996. Read on, for the rest of the story.

Addis Ababa is the headquarters of the United Nations Economic Commission for Africa (ECA). The ECA itself is one of five regional economic commissions across the world, which are part of a decentralized secretariat of the United Nations that has its headquarters in New York city. The other four regional commissions cover Europe, Western Asia, Asia and the Pacific, and Latin America and the Caribbean, with their respective headquarters in Geneva, Baghdad, Bangkok and Santiago de Chile.

On joining the United Nations, I realized at once that I was a small cog in a huge global wheel which revolved around New York city in the United States of America. All the staff of the United Nations secretariat owed allegiance to the Secretary-General, and they owed their professional loyalty not to any one state, or group of states, but to the collective membership of the United Nations. Moreover, it was made clear that an internationally recruited staff member, such as myself, could be assigned any responsibilities, and moved to any duty station in the world, at the Secretary-General's discretion.

This kind of orientation put me in a new frame of mind, peculiarly different from anything I had experienced before. It meant that in everything I did I was free to apply my best professional judgement, and recommend accordingly, free from the political dictates of any particular government, including my own. In this spirit, I devoted myself fully to the tasks before me, bringing my academic, practical and professional competence to bear on everything I did in the implementation of the ECA work programme.

At the end of two years, both the Chief of the Economic Cooperation Office, Mr Bax Nomvete, who was my immediate supervisor, and the Executive Secretary of ECA, Mr Adebayo Adedeji, were impressed by my work, and I was rated "Very Good" (or 2 on a scale of 1 to 6) in the official Performance Evaluation Report. Unknown to me, they had already contacted my Government to request that my contract be renewed for another two years. The government had readily agreed, and indicated that I could continue working for the U.N. for as long as my services were needed. This was exactly the green light that was needed to pave the way for my permanent employment in the organization.

I stayed with ECA for another three years, as Senior Economic Affairs Officer in the Economic Cooperation Office. Our office was charged with establishing five ECA sub-regional centres known as the Multinational Programming and Operational Centres. For a region as large as Africa, these sub-regional divisions were considered necessary if ECA was to make a tangible impact. With their headquarters in Tangier, Niamey, Yaounde, Kigali and Lusaka – these sub-regional centres served, respectively, the countries of North Africa, West Africa, Central Africa, the Great Lakes, and Eastern and Southern Africa, the largest sub-region of them all.

Based on our study of the economy of each sub-region, our office had the responsibility to formulate and oversee the implementation of appropriate multi-country programmes for each sub-region. The office also prepared the necessary documentation for meetings of officials and ministers at both the regional and sub-regional levels whenever the subject of multinational economic cooperation and integration was on the agenda.

I stayed with the ECA for three more years, performing my duties as best I could. My performance evaluations were now consistently rated 1, that is, "Excellent" or "Outstanding". I was determined to keep it up – as indeed I did – to the day of my retirement.

In 1983, the Chief of the Economic Cooperation Office, Mr Nomvete, reached retirement age and left the organization. From the time of my recruitment I had been his right hand man and close confidant, and I always acted as Officer in Charge whenever he was away from Addis Ababa. Everybody expected me to be his successor. Furthermore, I had already reached the top of my P-5 salary scale, and the D-1 level post left vacant by Mr Nomvete was the only promotional post available. I naturally aspired to be promoted to that post.

However, the Executive Secretary decided to side-step me. He gave the post to Mr Henri Bazin, a Haitian, who was also the Chief of the Trade Division.

Disappointed as I was, I took it calmly, trying, as usual, not to show it. But I felt convinced that it was now time for a change. From then on, I quietly resolved to look for another job, outside the ECA, but preferably within the United Nations system.

Then came a pleasant surprise. I was travelling on mission to Brazil, and the route from Addis Ababa was via Rome and New York. An old friend of mine, Professor Odero-Ogwel from Kenya, who once worked for the Sokoine University of Agriculture at Morogoro in Tanzania, but was presently with the United Nations World Food Council (WFC) in Rome, tipped me about an existing vacancy of Chief, Policy Development and Economic Analysis. He mentioned my name to his Executive Director, Mr. Maurice Williams, who arranged a brief interview with me on the day I touched down in Rome *en route* for New York. When the interview was over, the Executive Director asked me to stop by again on my return trip from Brazil.

On arrival in New York, I paid a brief call on Ms. Kate Starr Newell, who was Officer-in-Charge of the World Food Council Liaison Office located on the 29th floor of the U.N. Secretariat Building. Apart from its headquarters in Rome, and this liaison office in New York, the WFC had no office anywhere else in the world.

On my way back from Brazil, I stopped in Rome as planned, to be met with the happy news that the Executive Director of the WFC had decided to offer me the post of Chief, Policy Development and Economic Analysis, at the D-1 level. Imagine my delight! It had all happened so quickly I almost couldn't believe it. I had made no written application, provided no certificates, and no testimonials from my previous employer – nothing, in fact, except a short interview with the Executive Director, who was accompanied by his deputy, Mr. Diego de Gaspar, a Brazilian national.

I discovered later that there had been a letter of recommendation (copied to me in confidence) dated April 12, 1983, from Professor Bruce F. Johnston of the Food Research Institute, Stanford University, who was one of my doctoral supervisors, which recommended me highly for the post.

Said Johnston:

"It seems to me that in terms of professional training, experience, intelligence,   and personality, Temu would be extremely well qualified for the position of Chief of your Policy Development and Economic Analysis Section".

Incidentally, this particular post was exactly the same level of seniority as that of Chief, Economic Cooperation Office, in Addis Ababa to which the ECA Executive Secretary could have promoted me, had he wished. However, for me the post in Rome had more exciting prospects by far, not just because I would for the first time be working in Europe, but also because I would be working for a *new* U.N. agency, the World Food Council, and confronting new challenges. In other words, Mr Adedeji's refusal to promote me turned out to be a blessing in disguise.

The WFC Executive Director told me the job needed to be filled right away, but as both WFC and ECA were members of the same U.N. family, he knew pretty well it was going to be hard for me to break the news to my boss at ECA, let alone obtain a quick release from him. He therefore took it on himself to inform his ECA counterpart about it at a meeting of the executive heads of U.N. agencies which was scheduled to be held at New York Headquarters within a few days. I learned later that there were sharp exchanges between the two executive heads: with the ECA side accusing the WFC of 'poaching' a much-needed staff member from a sister agency, and the WFC side replying that the staff member 'poached' was joining WFC at a more senior level – a level to which ECA itself could easily have promoted him, if it had needed him that much.

Back at my office in Addis Ababa, my supervisor, Mr. Henri Bazin, who had already been briefed by the Executive Secretary, called me to his office. Though he congratulated me, he also expressed surprise that I should have applied for and been offered a job in the WFC without his knowledge. He informed me that the executive heads of the two agencies had met in New York and agreed that I was to continue at my job in Addis Ababa for the remaining three months to the end of the year, and report for duty in Rome at the beginning of January 1984.

Fortunately for me, the arrangement suited me perfectly. It allowed me the time I needed to wind up my affairs, both at ECA and back home in Tanzania where my wife and I were eager to bid farewell to our ageing parents. More importantly, it allowed us time to rearrange, as best we could, the schooling of our six children, the youngest of whom was in elementary school in Addis Ababa, the oldest in upper secondary school in England, with the others being at various schools in Kenya and Ethiopia.

Chapter V

1984 to 1986
At the United Nations World Food
Council, Rome, Italy

"... a most congenial working environment, where a small but vibrant team of professional staff worked happily together, under the exemplary leadership of a
soft-spoken American Executive Director, Mr. Maurice Williams".

On 2nd January 1984 I reported for work as Chief, Policy Development and Economic Analysis, at the headquarters of the United Nations World Food Council in Rome, Italy, and was accorded a warm welcome by the entire staff. The first thing that struck me was just how small WFC was compared with the ECA, or, for that matter, compared with the World Food Programme or the Food and Agriculture Organization (FAO), both of which had their headquarters in Rome. Having no office building of its own, the whole of the WFC secretariat occupied one corner on the third floor of the FAO building. The entire staff establishment of the WFC – professional, administrative and 'general service' – numbered 34 in all, that is, 31 in Rome, and 3 in New York.

Unlike typical U.N. agencies, WFC had no country representatives, and no country projects or field programmes of its own. The Council was just a deliberative body or policy making organ, not a substantive or operational one. Its high status was quite out of proportion to its size. This was due to the fact that it addressed global food and hunger issues *at the highest policy level*, and its staff served as the secretariat for a ministerial conference of 36 member states which convened once every three years. Its reports were submitted direct to the United Nations General Assembly for necessary action, which gave the Council a high political profile.

The policy issues addressed by the WFC, focusing as they did on the most perennial problem in the world – the elimination of hunger and malnutrition – were a practical and intellectual challenge, and remain so to this day. My colleagues and I were supposed to exercise our minds on these matters to the fullest. In the nature of our task, and given our staff resource limitations, our activities were not field-oriented, but depended more on in-depth desk research, and on insights gained from the work of other agencies and independent researchers.

My first three years with the Council were spent in Rome, in a most congenial working environment where a small but vibrant team of professional staff worked happily together, under the exemplary leadership of a soft-spoken American Executive Director, Mr. Maurice Williams. In keeping with our mandate, we organised a number of ministerial meetings in various world capitals such as Beijing, Addis Ababa, and Teheran, in each case reporting to the U.N. General Assembly.

Unfortunately, all was not well in our inter-agency relations. For quite some time –long predating my joining the Council – there had been a simmering dispute between the WFC and the FAO under its Director-General, Mr. Edouard Saouma, stemming from the overlapping functions of the two agencies. Food and nutrition were matters on the agenda of both agencies. The fine dividing line between the WFC as a ministerial policy organ, and the FAO as a specialised operational agency, had become increasingly blurred. After all, the FAO too had its own and much larger ministerial conference which formulated food policy and whose composition included the same ministers that attended the WFC conferences. The fact that the WFC reported to the General Assembly and the FAO to its own Ministerial Conference appeared to be an anomaly that only added to the confusion. This overlapping of functions between the tiny WFC and the giant FAO was now becoming an unbearable point of friction, with the WFC appearing more and more as a thorn in FAO's flesh.

By 1986, matters were coming to a head. Under pressure from the FAO, an increasing number of member states were clamouring for the abolition of the WFC. Among other things, they claimed that since its creation in 1974, the WFC had made little or no impact in eliminating global hunger. Unfortunately for the WFC, this period coincided with the time that Mr. Maurice Williams, the WFC Executive Director, who had staunchly stood his ground against the FAO, was leaving on retirement.

His Canadian successor, Mr Gerald Trant, was both too new and too weak to weather the storm. But before the inevitable happened, he made a last-ditch effort: he decided to strengthen the WFC Liaison Office in New York in the hope that it could more effectively lobby support for the Council from conference delegates and from resident ambassadors stationed at New York headquarters. In pursuit of this aim, and partly on my own behest, he decided to transfer me to New York to be the Director of the WFC Liaison Office in New York.

Chapter VI

1986 to 1991
At the World Food Council Liaison Office, United Nations Headquarters, New York.

"…fortune had smiled on me. The year 1986 –the year I turned 50 – still strikes a happy cord in my memory …
… Then, suddenly, everything changed. It was as if I had been struck by a thunderbolt!"

That I had always longed to work at the United Nations headquarters was no secret, and I welcomed the opportunity with open arms. Once again, it seemed that fortune had smiled on me. The year 1986 – the year I turned 50 – still strikes a happy cord in my memory. It was the year I reported for duty at the United Nations Secretariat in New York, with already nine years of U.N. service behind me, holding a permanent employment contract, and with a performance evaluation track record that left nothing to be desired.

My office in New York was located on the 29th floor of the U.N. Secretariat building, overlooking the East River. My family of eight lived in a cooperative apartment I had bought the year before at River House, Overlook Avenue, at Peekskill, in Westchester County, some 40 miles up the Hudson River. I would travel by Metro-North Railroad commuter train to Manhattan every morning on my way to work, and return home the same way in the evening at the end of the working day.

The office had only four staff members – Ms Newell, an American, who had been Officer-in-Charge prior to my arrival, two female secretaries, and myself. I was proud to be the supervisor of this small but well experienced and dedicated team. I felt confident that with determination we could meet any challenge.

During my first year in New York, the going was good. Ms Newell and I attended numerous meetings, and met and sensitized many diplomats and conference delegates about the role of the WFC. We kept the Executive Director in Rome constantly briefed about the goings-on in New York, and we prepared the ground for his frequent visits to New York and Washington, visits which would normally include a stop-over at his home in Canada. The Executive Director, for his part, appeared generally satisfied with our work. Occasionally, he and I would have lunch together, during which we would exchange ideas, and I would receive from him such instructions or recommendations as he considered helpful in the discharge of my functions.

Matters continued the same way for another year or so. I was beginning to feel that here at last was what I had always longed for – a nice comfortable job, with good remuneration and excellent retirement prospects, at a respectable level of seniority, working and interacting with professional colleagues (in the WFC secretariat as well as in the wider U.N. secretariat) with a common commitment and sense of purpose.

The WFC had no office elsewhere in the world, other than its headquarters in Rome, where I had already served, and its liaison office in New York where I was now serving. This made me feel that there was nothing to stop me staying on in New York until my retirement in eight years' time when, God willing, I would turn sixty. Consciously or unconsciously, plans for my future life were already evolving around that expectation.

Then, suddenly, everything changed. It was as if I had been struck by a thunderbolt! My boss – the Executive Director of the WFC – decided to fire me. In a letter dated 12 June 1989, copied to the top personnel boss, the Assistant Secretary-General, Office of Human Resources Management, Mr Kofi Annan, he listed several complaints, and then said to me: "I really feel that ... you might consider looking around in New York (or elsewhere) for another post by the end of the year". He ended his letter with a thinly veiled threat: "I would not like to take any decision which could damage you either professionally or personally, but..."

Chapter VII

A Threat To My Career

"Do not be afraid to fight injustice ... this is my legacy to posterity".

I was speechless. This was a letter from my boss. It was the last thing I had expected. What had I done? None of his complaints was true, or even made sense. But, whatever his reason or motive, I had to take the matter seriously. Overnight, all my dreams had been shattered. Any thoughts of a happy retirement from New York after eight years were put to an abrupt end, and replaced by one single preoccupation: how to *fight for my job.*

As I pondered my fate, memories of what had happened to me in 1975 in my own country, Tanzania, came back vividly to my mind. At that time, for no apparent reason, my boss had tried to kick me out of my job as National Planning Controller in the Ministry of Finance and Planning. I fought back, politely but firmly, and won. I was convinced that if I had not put up a fight, my career would have been ruined. Fortunately, I had fought it out, and achieved victory. Inspired by the memory of that experience, I now felt a rising tide of anger inside me, and I said – almost audibly – to myself, "I'll fight out this one too ... and *I'll win!*".

I recount this episode – indeed I am writing this book – in the interest of anyone who might find himself or herself, now or in the future, in a situation similar to mine. I regard this as my legacy to posterity. The moral is *not* that it pays to stand up in confrontation to your superiors. Rather, the point is that, far too often, subordinates in the workplace, when they are unjustly treated by their bosses, feel intimidated and tend to give in too easily without a fight, thereby ruining their careers and their future. For them, my story has a clear moral: *do not be afraid to fight injustice,* particularly when it is clear that it is being perpetrated out of sheer malice.

Let me say, in parenthesis, that I had always had the highest regard for both the Permanent Secretary (my Tanzanian boss in the Ministry) and for Mr Gerald Trant (my Canadian boss who was the WFC Executive Director). Indeed, I had a lingering hope that I might one day meet them again in later life, preferably after we were all comfortably retired. Had that happened, we would have renewed old friendships, cracked a few jokes, recalled old fights between the boss and the underdog, and let bygones be bygones. Unfortunately – as fate would have it – they have both been dead for some years now. May their souls rest in peace!

The fight for my job began in earnest in mid-1989. The Executive Director had given me till the end of 1989 to quit the Council. He even stopped giving me assignments. This left me free to exercise my mind solely on two issues: first, what to do to save my job; and second, how to find an alternative job, in case my efforts to save my present one failed.

Day in and day out, I would commute as usual by Metro-North Railroad between my home in Peekskill, Westchester County, and Grand Central station in mid-Manhattan. From there, I would walk to my office at One U.N. Plaza. At the office, staff morale was now at its lowest. Ms. Newell and I were barely on talking terms. Clearly, the contents of the so-called personal and confidential letter to me had been leaked, and were now common knowledge, if not common talk, in the U.N. corridors. My adversaries were jubilant, my sympathisers pitiful. All of them knew that my days were numbered. I had been shown the door!

The year 1990 is exactly the year in which, had the Executive Director had his way, I would have packed my bags and bade an unceremonious farewell to the United Nations. Instead, it turned out – not by accident but by very purposeful design – to be the busiest and most creative year in the entire history of my international service.

Three things preoccupied my mind and prompted everything that I did. My first preoccupation was to keep watch on the Executive Director. I knew he would resort to all sorts of manoeuvres in an effort to be rid of me; and I was determined to match – if possible outmatch – every move of his with a counter-move of mine. Convinced that it was now or never, I had to be constantly on the alert, ready to fight him every step of the way. I was not going to be caught off guard, and wake up one morning to find that my 'separation from the service' was a *fait accompli*. I knew that such a possibility always existed, and I had to do all I could to forestall it.

My second preoccupation was to ensure that I had to do something positive – call it image building, or *re-building*, if you like. This meant that I had to involve myself in some visible activity, or activities, of value to the United Nations, as a standing demonstration to anyone that I was still able and willing to perform my duties competently and creatively, unscathed by the scandal that surrounded me. It was a way of keeping my morale high.

My third preoccupation, of course, and by far the most important, was to prepare to fight, tooth and nail, the Executive Director himself, taking maximum advantage of the excellent legal services of my friend and counsel, Mr Thomas Dube of Zimbabwe. The fortifying responses I kept receiving from my high-level contacts provided me with the moral ammunition I needed to wage the legal struggle confidently.

The fact that my fight along these three fronts was so successful was due, in large part, to the sympathy and cooperation I received from my friends and colleagues, inside as well as outside the United Nations. In what follows, a few examples will be cited in special tribute to them.

In addition to being high-handed and arbitrary, there was something particularly offensive about the Executive Director's decision to deprive me of my post, which I wanted to see exposed – the decision was *discriminatory.*

Accordingly, on 28 August 1989 I called on Mr. Mahmud M. Suqi, Co-ordinator of the United Nations Panel on Discrimination and Other Grievances, to explain my case to him. I informed him of my intention to bring my case before his Panel, to which he readily agreed. Two weeks later, on 11 September 1989, I submitted the following to the Panel:

"Subject: Discriminatory action by Management in depriving me of my permanent post

I appreciate the opportunity you gave me of discussing my case with you on Monday, 28 August. I left with you the following documents:

1. Mr. Trant's letter to me, dated 28 July 1989, notifying me that it had been   determined I be placed against a transitional post;

2. Letter from Mr. Annan to Mr. Trant, dated 12 July 1989;

3. Letter from Mr, Trant to Mr. Annan, dated 13 June 1989, to which was attached a copy of Mr. Trant's letter to me, dated 12 June 1989;

4. Copy of my letter to Mr. Annan , dated 21 July 1989, to which was attached a copy of my interim reply, dated 18 July 1989 to Mr. Trant's letter of 12 June 1989;

5. WFC staffing table dated 1 September 1986, the date Mr. Trant assumed office, and another (unofficial) dated 22 August 1989 reflecting the current position.

Today, I am attaching a sixth document, namely the letter from Mr. Kofi Annan to me, dated 6 September 1989 which I have just received. This letter, which had been expected, completes and formalizes the action described in Mr. Trant's letter of 28 July 1989. The letter has finally lifted the curtain by revealing to me, for the first time, the pretext used to deprive me of my post. (Mr.Trant of course never cared to tell me the reason for his decision in his peremptory note of 28 July 1989). He left it to me to learn it all through the "system", as I have just done, one and a half months later.

According to Mr. Annan's letter, Mr Trant has informed him that he is abolishing my post at the Liaison Office as part of the retrenchment exercise.

Now, I know what the retrenchment exercise is all about, and what rules govern its implementation. I also know that Mr. Trant, as executive head, is in the privileged position to shuffle and re-shuffle his staff to suit his preferences. But this privilege, delegated to him by the Secretary-General, was never intended to be exercised arbitrarily, much less abused.

I say this because:

(a) There is evidence that the Executive Director wanted to take my post away long before he ever thought of abolishing the post at the Liaison Office in New York;

(b) My post has not in fact been abolished but simply taken away and given to another staff member. You can see this from the staffing tables I left with you;

(c) If his reason for my removal was indeed the lack of a post, I should have been   given a fair chance, on an open and competitive basis, for consideration for all the remaining D-1 positions in the Council. The vacancy management and staff redeployment process actually requires this. Only thus can justice be seen to have been done.

In addition, I appeal to your respected Panel to consider the following circumstances:

(a) That the World Food Council secretariat does not have a single African on the general service staff;

(b) That the World Food Council secretariat will not have a single African on the professional staff after my departure;

(c) That after six years of service at the D-1 level, I am the most senior of the present D-1's on the World Food Council secretariat, second in seniority only to the Executive Director;

(d) My consistently high standard of performance during 12 years of service to the United Nations at senior officer and principal officer levels;

(e) The Executive Director's malicious letter about me dated 13 June 1989 sent openly to the Assistant Secretary-General of the Office of Human Resources Management but deliberately kept unknown to me.

I also request your Panel to note that in his "reorganization" of the Council secretariat, the Executive Director has created new titles for the existing D-1 positions, for which I should have been eligible to compete, in order to confuse people. The Chief, Policy Development and Economic Analysis (a position I encumbered for three years before my reassignment to New York) is re-titled "Special Representative of the Executive Director", a title normally reserved for special representatives of the Secretary-General. The Chief, Policy Co-ordination and External Relations, to whom my present post is being given, is re-styled "Acting Deputy Executive Director" which creates the impression that he has been promoted, although no promotion has occurred and no substantive post of Deputy Executive Director even exists on the establishment to which he could be appointed, or aspire to be appointed, in an acting capacity.

In my humble view, these organizational manoeuvres, which were invented and kept in great secrecy until announced, are an additional factor which helps to disguise the discriminatory nature of the action which the Executive Director has taken against me. I leave it to your distinguished Panel to judge whether his decision to take away my permanent and pensionable post is in the interest of the World Food Council or of the United Nations; and also whether the way he has dealt with me as one of his senior staff members is fair and square.

As I appeal to your distinguished Panel for a redress of my grievances, I should like to take this opportunity to pledge my full co-operation with it in all its investigations."

Incidentally, whatever indirect pressure my appeal to the Panel Against Discrimination and Other Grievances (in September 1989) may have brought to bear on my main case, this particular appeal was never actually heard. The good thing is, the entire record of my submission was already available as a relevant input by the time when (in July 1990) the major appeal to the Joint Appeals Board was launched.

Chapter VIII

Keeping a watchful eye on the Executive Director.

"Programme managers throughout the United Nations were doing this,
often with good intentions, but occasionally,
as in my case, in order to get rid of a staff member they did not like"

Knowing his ill intentions, it was not hard for me to imagine the kind of administrative manoeuvres – so-called 'personnel actions'- the Executive Director might invoke, using his privileged position as my boss. I suspected that one of his first personnel actions would be to take advantage of an ongoing United Nations system-wide staff reduction and retrenchment exercise. The situation offered him an ideal opportunity to drop me quietly without any hairs being raised. It was a mere budgetary exercise: you only needed to remove me from my securely funded 'core' post and place me against a 'non-core' post slated to be abolished at the end of the year. It was that simple! Programme managers throughout the United Nations were doing this, mostly with good intentions, but occasionally, as in my case, in order to get rid of a staff member they didn't like.

As it turned out, I was perfectly right. My Executive Director tried to do just that. Indeed he did worse: he did it behind my back, *while I was away on home leave.* It was as if he wanted to enjoy the drama of catching me unawares. Even after my return from home leave, he continued to keep me in the dark by hiding the relevant documents from me, until I discovered them later purely by accident. And when I did, I dropped a bombshell! I took strong exception to his unethical tactics, and I was later on to cite it in my appeal to the JAB Panel as evidence that the Executive Director had been acting in bad faith.

In a strongly worded letter to the Assistant Secretary-General for Human Resource Management, Mr Kofi Annan, dated 21 February 1990, I queried:

> *"Exactly why must the Executive Director's actions be so shrouded in secrecy? Of all things, a P.5 personnel action, once completed, is supposed to be furnished immediately to the staff member affected by such action. It is not to be handled as if it was a secret death warrant! Where is the transparency which we talk of in the United Nations, an organization which the world regards as the custodian and arch-guardian of human rights?"*

The Executive Director's next move was to prepare an official Performance Evaluation Report (PER) intended to provide supporting documentary evidence for his allegation that I was unfit for my job. Such a PER had been expected and was long overdue. In normal circumstances this would have provided him with powerful ammunition, sufficient to deal my career a fatal blow.

But the circumstances were far from normal. For one thing, the timing was all wrong. Unfortunately for the Executive Director, his 'performance evaluation' came *after* he had already announced his intention to fire me. I was quick to point out that this was a deplorable 'sentence first, verdict later' dictatorial tactic, and that it was further evidence of the Executive Director's bad faith.

In addition, the PER itself was full of loopholes and inconsistencies, which I vividly exposed. The result was that his PER never saw the light of day: it lost all credibility and never became part of my official personnel record. In short, it was totally rejected by the Administration.

The submission of a formal rebuttal of my Performance Evaluation Report by the Executive Director for the period 1 November 1986 to 31 December 1988 was made, and with good reason, well before my appeal to the Joint Appeals Board. That PER had been fabricated by the Executive Director, hurriedly and belatedly, the moment he realized that he needed documentary evidence to support his decision to expel me from the World Food Council. Knowing this, I took quick pre-emptive action: no sooner did the PER appear than I attacked it in a hard-hitting rebuttal, which I submitted on 20 February 1990.

This meant that by July 1990, when the JAB started to consider my appeal, the Panel already had full knowledge of my rebuttal of the Executive Director's PER. I believe they found my rebuttal quite convincing, which probably explains why, when it came to the crux, the Panel took such a short time to reach a unanimous verdict in my favour. Apparently, the Panel saw no need to interview me for cross examination, or to call witnesses, or even to require my counsel, Mr Thomas Dube (who was always on standby), to appear before it.

While neither my written appeal to the JAB, nor the JAB report itself, makes any mention of the PER, there is little doubt that the PER and its rebuttal (like my appeal against discrimination) must have influenced the Panel's thinking considerably, and conditioned its attitude favourably towards me. My legal counsel also had the benefit of the rebuttal in preparing the formal appeal to the JAB, though he too would not cite it.

It would seem that both the rebuttal itself and its timing were absolutely crucial. The full text of the rebuttal was as follows:

"Rebuttal of the Performance Evaluation Report for the period 1 November 1986 –31 December 1988

(Submitted on 20 February 1990)

"My Executive Director is telling the world, 'I hate Temu, and I don't want anybody to employ him' ".

(a) Introduction and summary

1. I have kept this rebuttal short because two other investigations against the   Executive Director relating to me are under way. One is before the Panel Against Discrimination and Other Grievances. It is a complaint against the Executive Director for singling me out for discriminatory treatment among the D-1 staff. The other is a pending appeal to the Joint Appeals Board against a decision to take away my permanent post arbitrarily and handing it out to a staff member of his choice.

2. These two investigations are clearly related to this disputed Performance Evaluation Report (PER), and hence to the rebuttal, if for no other reason than that this PER was prepared by the Executive Director <u>after,</u> and not before, he had taken these questionable decisions, in order to try to provide retrospective justification for them.

3 Turning to the PER itself, I would summarise my case as follows: my single most important complaint is that the present PER is totally lacking in objectivity and fairness. It is replete with inconsistencies, some of them of a gross kind. In the first place, I find the report completely inconsistent with any report that has ever been made on me in the past – anywhere, any

time, by any supervisor under whom I have worked, in or out of the United Nations, in any capacity whatsoever.

4. Secondly, the report is inconsistent – much too inconsistent – with the Executive Directors own preceding report, made a little over two years ago.

5. Thirdly, there are strange internal inconsistencies even within the present PER itself which cast serious doubt on the Executive Director's good faith and sincerity, and gives it the appearance of a personal vendetta.

6. Taken together, these three types of inconsistencies, of which there are glaring examples which I shall pin-point, call into question the credibility or sincerity of the report.

7. Finally, actions taken by the Executive Director prior to, and outside the context of, this PER, to which we can only allude cursorily, confirm the impression that this PER is part of a pattern deliberately designed to discredit me and throw me out of the U.N. It is simply not a genuine performance evaluation of my work.

(b) Inconsistencies between the present performance evaluation report and all_previous evaluation reports.

8. It is my humble submission that the inconsistency between the PER of this supervisor on the one hand, and the PERs of all my previous supervisors on the other, goes far beyond anything that could reasonably be explained by the fact that different supervisors think differently. Even in this sphere of human life, where personal value judgements count for so much, there is at least a certain minimum stability. Human behaviour cannot be so erratic. I fail to understand how, for no

apparent reason, anyone's character or performance can change so drastically and suddenly as mine is being alleged to have changed. Were behaviour so erratic, would the performance evaluation system itself be worth anything for purposes of tracking a staff member's career development or of evaluating his genuine progress?

9. Consider my particular case. This PER says that I am a man who cannot work independently. It rates me D. It comments: "Needs close supervision". As the panel will note, over the past 12 years, all previous reports have rated me A, and seldom B. Surely, the choice before the panel is whether to believe all my previous supervisors – the last of whom, Mr. Maurice J. Williams, has just written a moving testimonial to two heads of U.N. agencies to recommend me for a senior position – or to disregard all of them and believe only the present incumbent who is technically my supervisor but who actually lives in Italy, visits New York occasionally, and claims to supervise a D-1 staff member of proven experience whose responsibilities, in their very nature, are not even amenable to supervision in the first place.

10. Ask the head of any U.N. agency and he will confirm to you that someone running a liaison office located in New York cannot be effectively supervised by a boss based thousands of miles away in Rome, Geneva, Nairobi, Santiago or Bangkok. My Executive Director of course knows this. He knows in his heart that I have been working independently, that I have successfully defended and transformed the image of the WFC liaison office, if not the Council itself, before the CPC, the ECOSOC Special Commission, and personalities

in New York, from a time when there was a clamour for its abolition and absorption by FAO, to the present time when it is widely respected, and criticism of it, if any, is completely muted. The last three years during which I have been in New York have been entirely crucial, if not decisive, for all agencies with liaison offices here, including the WFC. It has been a trying time, when one has had to stand up before powerful bodies to explain, clarify and convince. Anyone who knows my Executive Director understands that he would not have tolerated my presence in New York for one moment, let alone for three critical years, if he did not believe that I was doing a good job. Yet he has secretly written to the Assistant Secretary-General/Office of Human Resources and Management, Mr. Kofi Annan, in a letter dated 13 June 1989 to say, "Temu has not been successful in representing the Council or the Council's interests". If that is true, am I still in New York, at the end of three years, drawing a D-1 salary at the United Nation's expense, simply because of the benevolence of his heart?

11. I ask the panel to bear in mind that "Needs close supervision" and similar slurs such as "No useful initiative during period" are being made of an officer at D-1 level, who was appointed by the Secretary-General to be Officer-in-Charge of the Council before this Executive Director assumed office, who joined the U.N. at P-5 level 12 years ago, and who before that time had, in his own country, been Director of the Economic Research Bureau at the University of Dar es Salaam, supervising research academicians; National Planning Controller at the Ministry of Finance and Planning in charge of a team of

professional economists; and Director of the Institute of Finance Management producing professional accountants, bankers and insurers. Today, at 53 years of age, in a little-known office with only one female professional at P-4, I am abruptly being pronounced in need of close supervision, lacking in initiative, not bringing my knowledge to bear on my work, little known to anyone, producing only a few useful pieces of written work! If this is all that I am good for, how did I ever get recruited into the United Nations, let alone stay there? These are not genuine comments by a responsible supervisor. They are insults. My Executive Director is telling the world, "I hate Temu and I don't want anybody to employ him",

12. I do not need to multiply these examples. The panel can examine the record before it and decide for itself whether to believe or disregard the Executive Director's ratings and comments on other attributes of my performance, particularly competence, quality of work, initiative, and working relations – all of which, without exception, contrast sharply in tone and substance from all previous reports, including, <u>ironically</u>, the Executive Director's own preceding report, to which I now turn.

© **Inconsistencies between the present performance evaluation report and the preceding one by the same Executive Director.**

13. This second category of contradictions, coming as they do from the same man, reporting on the same individual, within such a short time span, is so incomprehensible to me that it has led me, however reluctantly, to accuse the Executive Director of having some hidden motive for wishing to boot me out of

the Council. I would not have appealed to the Panel Against Discrimination and other Grievances if I did not believe this sincerely.

14. Comments by me would be superfluous. Let the panel itself put both reports side by side, read across, and draw its own conclusions.

15. However, please permit me, if I may, to make two observations. Firstly, it is problematic enough when reports on the same individual by different supervisors are sharply at variance. But when the <u>same</u> supervisor, in a short period of time, changes his mind so completely, one is entitled to wonder whether such a dramatic change may not be as much a reflection of the supervisor's own change of attitude, as it is a reflection of the supposed change in the performance of the staff member.

16. Secondly, the inconsistencies between the Executive Director's first and second reports go way beyond what could reasonably be explained by the fact of my having taken a new assignment at a new duty station. I flatly deny that my work performance has deteriorated because of changed assignments or duty stations, as the Executive Director would like us to believe.

17. In this connection, I would point out that this is not the first time I have changed duty stations. Nor is it the first time I have been assigned new responsibilities. Members of the panel have only to glance at my C.V. to see that I have held responsible positions, at a high level, in and out of the United Nations, for over 16 years continuously. In the course of that period, I have changed assignments six times, and duty stations four times, spanning three continents – having worked in Dar es Salaam, Tanzania; Addis Ababa, Ethiopia; Rome,

Italy; and now New York. Each time my capacity for change and adaptation to new situations while discharging new (and often higher) responsibilities has been amply demonstrated. The change from Dar es Salaam to Addis Ababa when I first entered the United Nations was a drastic one, involving a new and hard location and entailing entirely new responsibilities in very trying social, economic and security circumstances. Yet my performance in ECA was officially rated excellent from the beginning. The change, six years later, from ECA in Addis Ababa to WFC in Rome, involving an inter-agency transfer, the assumption of totally new responsibilities (again at a higher level), and living and working for the first time in a non-English speaking environment, was another drastic change. Yet, my performance there was rated <u>A</u> by the then Executive Director, Mr. Maurice J. Williams, during the entire period that I served under him.

18. Why should this latest switch from Rome to New York, at a time when my experience has fully matured, a switch moreover to an English-speaking country with which I have had the closest ties and affinity from the time twenty years ago when I studied here as a graduate and a doctoral student – why, I ask, should this particular move so totally and negatively transform my character and my performance in the eyes of the present Executive Director? How and why can I so totally have failed, in this special case, to adjust to my new working environment or to my new work responsibilities? Let the panel be the judge.

(d) Inconsistencies within the present PER itself.

19. The third category of contradictions, as the panel will no doubt have noticed, is evident <u>within</u> the very report which is under dispute.

20. For example, is it not odd for the Executive Director to specifically comment that my attitude to the United Nations is "Very Positive", and that I have a "solid academic background and considerable relevant experience", and yet claim that I do not bring this background and experience to bear on WFC activities? Is this because I am unable or unwilling to do so? If unable, why does he admit that I have a "solid academic background and considerable relevant experience"? If unwilling, why then does he say that my attitude to the U.N. is "very positive"? Which of his statements are we supposed to believe?

21. Secondly, if the Executive Director honestly means and believes in the ratings and comments he has awarded me in Section III of the PER he cannot logically rate me "A good Performance" under Section IV. To do so is dishonest and hypocritical, and it deceives no one. Whoever reads the report seriously will understand that the actual ratings in Section III and the accompanying slurs (to call them 'comments' is a mere euphemism), admit of only one conclusion – "An Unsatisfactory Performance" . Perhaps the only reason the reporting officer does not say so – unless it was just to coat the pill with sugar – is in order to save himself the trouble of having to provide a written explanation for his remarks, as required by the regulations, something he surely would have found extremely difficult to do.

22. I humbly request the panel to recognise that there is a great deal more to this PER than meets the eye. Its message is subtle and brutal. The ratings in Section III tell the real story. They have to be considered not only alongside the wry comments made by the reporting officer but also against any favourable comments he should have made but refrained from making. Without question, the message of this PER is extremely damaging and was intended to be so. If the authorities at Headquarters had taken it literally, or taken the Executive Director's secret letters to the Assistant Secretary-General/Office of Human Resources Management literally, I would not be here today. And if this is going only by his written word, I shudder to imagine what he may have communicated orally behind my back!

(e) Other inconsistencies.

23. As a further test of the Executive Director's credibility, the panel may wish to satisfy itself as to why, if my performance in New York is so bad, and my performance in Rome so good – both according to the Executive Director's own assessment – why has the Executive Director not transferred me back to Rome, considering that during this very period he has been busy, and has kept OHRM officials busy, searching for qualified candidates to fill no less than four senior vacancies? I have, in fact, at least twice in writing proposed just that, but he has not responded, because his single-minded aim has been to boot me out of the Council.

Lest the panel thinks I am imputing motives by casting doubt on the good intentions of my Executive Director, I invite the panel to read the Executive Director's own letter dated June

13, 1989 which he sent <u>secretly</u> to the Assistant Secretary-General/Office of Human Resources Management, Mr. Kofi Annan, In it he requests Mr. Annan to find me an alternative job, but he also tells him: "Temu is operating at a level closer to a P-3 rather than D-1". In other words, he is saying, in one and the same breath, "Find Temu a job", and "Do not employ Temu because he is unfit". His message has no other possible interpretation. This is not just inconsistency, it is malice especially when one considers that such a letter is sent to the top Personnel Boss behind my back. And this by a man who once had occasion to lecture me over my junior colleague on the need for transparency in the United Nations!

24. I believe that this episode can assist the panel in understanding what kind of a reporting officer we have to contend with. More than that, it shows the panel that this PER is but the tip of the iceberg, and that the real reason for the nature, tone, substance and timing of this PER lies elsewhere and may have little to do with any genuine evaluation of my work performance. Once this veil is lifted, all the apparent inconsistencies described in the rebuttal can easily be explained as part of a pattern designed to discredit me.

(f) Postscript to the rebuttal.

In conclusion, I request your distinguished panel to consider the inherent limitations of the present performance evaluation system in those cases where the first reporting officer, the second reporting officer, and the Executive Head, are one and the same person. There is no go-between to restrain him when his emotions are aroused. If there had been, it would have ensured more objectivity, more consistency, more sanity, and certainly more honesty, in the evaluation. It certainly would have prevented a situation such as this one whereby my Executive Director, completely unchecked, smears my name, takes major decisions against me unilaterally, and even attempts to take away my post – and only then decides to produce a so-called Performance Evaluation Report which is suitably tailored to justify the damage he has already done. These 'sentence first, verdict later' dictatorial tactics of the Executive Director are among the subject of my complaints elsewhere, and it seems to me that they are possible only because the first reporting officer, the second reporting officer, and the Executive Head are all rolled in one.

25. It is also relevant to consider the peculiar problems associated with small agencies of which your panel is no doubt aware. By any standards WFC, though politically influential and headed by an ASG-grade appointee, is a tiny agency, consisting of a maximum of twelve professionals – a minuscule compared, say, with FAO or WFP which have Divisions or even Sections, never mind Departments, which are larger than WFC. Many people are unaware that the World Food Council bears no resemblance, except in name, to the World Food Programme. This has often led one to question whether such a small agency need really have a liaison office of its own in New York, considering that the liaison offices of some other agencies located here are nearly equal in size to the entire WFC. It is only natural that in an agency so small, when frictions develop and mutual confidence among the staff becomes eroded, some bizarre and irrational things can happen. I see myself as a victim of this unfortunate circumstance.

CHAPTER IX

PROTECTING MY PROFESSIONAL IMAGE.

"I was determined to hold my head high, to keep my professional image intact..."

Protection of one's professional image is an exercise in confidence building, a way of keeping one's morale high. That was something I needed now more than ever before. I figured that if other people had a positive image of me, and were impressed by my work, that alone would be sufficient to boost my self-esteem. The converse, of course, was also true: a negative image by others would be ruinous to my self-confidence, which is exactly what the Executive Director wanted. But I would not let that happen. I was determined to hold my head high, to keep my professional image intact – to fortify my moral edifice, which I knew had strong pillars, and stood on a solid foundation.

My educational attainment and an excellent performance evaluation track record of my work constituted my solid foundation; and my existing "pillars" were none other than my various high-level contacts, in and out of the United Nations, that I knew I could count on to vouch for me.

In pursuit of this aim, I contacted several high-level executives whom I briefed about my situation, and to whom I readily offered my services, if needed. I must confess that I was extremely heartened to see just how encouraging and sympathetic most of their responses were. This gave me the impression that even if I was booted out of the WFC, I would have little difficulty finding an alternative job, whether within or outside the United Nations. It was extremely good to feel that way!

By way of tribute, I like to cite a few examples to illustrate the kinds of sentiments expressed by several senior executives, which I found most reassuring.

"As the Council's Chief for policy development and economic analysis Peter Temu consistently made an excellent contribution. He directed the work on African agriculture and food problems at a critical stage in that continent's policy review, redirection and structural adjustment. He is a fine economist and his work was of high professional quality and policy responsiveness"

--Maurice Williams
Former Executive Director, WFC
September 26, 1989

"This is to confirm our understanding that…the services of Mr Peter Temu [will be made] available to DIESA for the rest of this year, to the extent that his assignments for you permit. We would wish to have Mr Temu work on subjects of food and agriculture and would consider him our WFC/DIESA Advisor on Food Security"

--Goran Ohlin
Officer-in-Charge
Department of International Economic and Social Affairs
United Nations Headquarters
March 1, 1990

"... I want you to know how much I appreciate your interest and you may be sure that it will receive full consideration as we begin the process of assembling our team"

--Maurice F. Strong
Secretary-General
United Nations Conference on Environment and Development
March 12, 1990

"I appreciated greatly your comments on the materials I shared with you... Your kind references to President Carter were also well taken. His personal vision and leadership sustain and inspire 'Project Africa'. And I agree wholeheartedly with your observation that the world needs people like him to throw their weight behind the crusade against hunger"

--Jeffrey Clark
Director, 'Project Africa'
The Carter Center of Emory University
June 21, 1990

"Our entire initiative certainly cannot make the impact it should unless the preparation of the groundwork is sufficiently thorough. We can think of no one more qualified than Mr Temu to take up this challenging task"

--Basem Khader
Officer-in-Charge
UNDP Regional Bureau for Africa
October 11, 1991

"Your letter to the Secretary-General of the OAU...is a testimony to our common   desire to work towards the eradication of hunger and

malnutrition...I would like to thank you for the vibrant statement
that you made on 15th September 1989..."

...Oumarou G. Youssoufou
Ambassador and Executive Secretary of the OAU to the United
Nations
September 21, 1989

These few communications underlie my desire, at the peak of the crisis, to maintain both diplomatic and professional rapport at a high level. The tone and substance of these complimentary remarks by high-level executives will indicate to the reader the satisfaction I must have felt in seeing that there were some well-placed and sympathetic guys out there on whose understanding and generosity I could count, should the worst come to the worst. I felt confident that I was not alone. To all intents and purposes, I had succeeded in protecting my professional image which the Executive Director had sought so hard to destroy.

But there was another and more substantive side to my efforts to create professional rapport: it entailed my actual participation in professional activities of various sorts *outside* the scope of the WFC. Naturally, this aspect grew in importance as my work assignments within WFC dwindled. That probably explains why my involvement in extra-WFC activities reached a peak around 1990, which is precisely when my Executive Director stripped me of my role as Chief of the WFC Liaison Office in New York and would no longer assign me any substantive work.

I complained bitterly at the way I was being made to appear redundant, while all my colleagues were grossly overworked and forced to do without my professional contribution. On 29 May 1990, a two-page letter from me to the Executive Director stated, in part –

"…it is sad to reflect that throughout the entire 'WFC year' from 1 June 1989 to 31 May 1990, during which four substantive regional workshops were organised by the Council, followed by the WFC Ministerial session just ended in Bangkok, you did not see fit to involve me in any of these five major activities, in any capacity whatsoever. Whatever your reasons may be, I would be less than candid if I did not say that I am amazed at the number of times you thought it necessary to send colleagues from Rome at great expense to attend meetings in and around New York, Washington or Canada, despite my presence here. With respect to Canada, it surprises me that despite its proximity to New York, you have chosen to exclude me totally, during my three and a half years at this duty station, from participation in any official mission to that country – a country which has always been a staunch supporter of the Council, and whose capital is located so conveniently close to New York. By contrast, visits to Canada by colleagues travelling all the way from Rome have been frequent".

This letter so infuriated the Executive Director that he could not bring himself to answer it. Instead, he passed it over to his Executive Officer, a relatively junior Italian official called Giuliano Comba, to reply. Mr Comba said to me, among other things, that "the prerogative of deciding whether WFC will be represented at a meeting and by whom rests with the Executive Director".

My answer to Mr Comba was that he had replied to a letter "that I never did write". Then, as if to educate a novice, I said to him –

"My best advice to you would be that next time you have to reply to someone else's letter on the Executive Director's behalf, which is a privilege for you, please be particularly careful to read the letter yourself in order to be sure you understand its meaning, and, if in doubt, check with the Executive Director or with the writer himself to find out exactly what they are talking about. Written communications to the Executive Director from his senior colleagues on matters of this kind are better thought out than you may think.

I trust you will find these suggestions useful in your future work"

After this caustic sarcasm, it should not surprise anyone that Mr Comba never wrote to me again, until he finally left the Council in March 1992, without bidding me good bye!

Chapter X

Self-assignments.

"I would portray him as the originator of every good idea, and as always the boss calling the shots. I knew this was good for his ego..."

Once it became clear that my boss had no intention giving me any meaningful assignment, my strategy and tactics changed appropriately. My first objective was to ensure that at any given time I would always have, and be seen to have, one or more substantive pieces of work – or self-assignments – that were both constructive and of direct relevance to the WFC's activities. My second objective was to figure out how to secure my Executive Director's approval for whatever I wished to do, knowing that even though such approval might only be reluctantly given, or even denied, protocol still demanded that I should seek it. It would serve no useful purpose, and it might be counter-productive, were I to try to 'go it alone' in defiance of the Executive Director's wishes, and I was not about to commit such a blunder.

Naturally, my attention now focussed on activities that I could carry out away from my office desk at the WFC liaison office, of which I was no longer the chief. I could not stand the humiliation of working under Ms Kate Newell, the junior official that had until yesterday been my subordinate, whom I had severely reprimanded for indiscipline, but who had now won the Executive Director's favour to be appointed Acting Chief..

Away from my office desk, one of the first assignments I sought was to collaborate with fellow economists in relevant U.N. departments in New York. In this connection, I recall with gratitude the sympathetic ear and cordial welcome I received from the late Mr Goran Ohlin, the Assistant Secretary-General and head of the Department of International Economic and Social Affairs (DIESA).

Following my discussions with him and his contacts with my Executive Director, he addressed a letter to Mr Trant, dated 1 March 1990, which stated, in part:

> *"This is to confirm our understanding that … we would wish to have Mr. Peter Temu work on subjects of food and agriculture and would consider him our WFC/DIESA Advisor on Food Security.*
>
> *This is considered an informal arrangement requiring no administrative action. I hope this is agreeable to you"*

Having obtained the green light from the WFC Executive Director, Mr Ohlin then introduced me to his immediate subordinate, Mr Cristian Ossa, Director of General Analysis and Policies Division, with whom we had the closest professional collaboration.

The next assignment I conjured up for myself concerned the International Food Policy Research Institute (IFPRI) whose activities were well in line with my own professional interests and also within the WFC's mandate. IFPRI was located away from New York, in Washington DC, and for that reason alone, I thought it the ideal place for me to go to. The more time I could spend away from New York the better. Initially, I sought permission to stay at IFPRI for three months, but in the end I was authorised to stay for only one month – April 1990 – which I utilized most productively.

However, securing permission to move to IFPRI was no easy task. The Executive Director knew – and I could easily read his mind – that my presence there would give me more professional visibility than he would have wished. For that reason, I went about it with the utmost caution, determined not to fail.

More than ever, it was necessary *not* to tread on the Executive Director's sensitive toes. In all the official contacts I made, I would portray him as the originator of every good idea, and as always the boss calling the shots. I knew this was good for his ego, and I had made it my habit to do so every time I wanted to elicit a favour from him. My IFPRI proposal was a test case. I began by citing an agreement which the Executive Director himself had signed not long before with the Director of IFPRI on the need for mutual collaboration between the two institutions. Next, I craftily made it appear that it was he who was taking the initiative towards its implementation. I then drafted for his signature a suitably worded memo from himself to his opposite number, the IFPRI Director, giving the impression that I was being posted to IFPRI on his orders, much like an errand boy.

The memo I drafted for him ran as follows:

"On my instructions, Peter Temu, my Senior Policy Advisor, will already have contacted you about his impending three-month assignment at IFPRI. In the spirit of our joint memorandum signed by you on 9 February 1988, and by me on 3 March 1988, I believe that Temu's exposure to and interaction with IFPRI would yield valuable dividends for WFC as well as for IFPRI.

I propose that initially Temu stays with IFPRI for three months, March through May. During that time, he will also interact with other

Washington-based experts, particularly in the World Bank and IMF, dealing with African food and agricultural problems – an area in which I have given him a specific assignment.

*If you are agreeable, we can leave the details and **modus operandi** to be thrashed out between him and your own colleagues, with whom I understand he is already in contact.*

I take it that IFPRI will agree to provide him with office accommodation, secretarial assistance and access to the usual research facilities, while WFC will continue to take care of his remuneration.

Please let me know if you concur with these arrangements so that we can give the necessary green light"

My tactics worked. I had found the right words to put in his mouth, including the royal "we". The letter was reproduced verbatim and despatched under his signature in the form of a telex from the WFC Director in Rome to the Director of IFPRI in Washington D.C. That way, I managed to get the green light I needed to move to Washington. To me, that was all that mattered. However, my Executive Director would not let me stay there for a whole three months. That would give me too much freedom. In the event, I ended up spending the whole month of April 1990 at IFPRI, during which I lived happily with the staff, working on an assignment that was of topical relevance to both IFPRI and the WFC, i.e. an examination of what food strategies are appropriate for African countries,

The report I produced at the end of this assignment, entitled "African National Food Strategies – A Suggested Approach", was well received, even applauded, by many who read it, if not by the Executive Director himself. For me, it certainly served its intended purpose, namely, giving me professional visibility before my colleagues in the United Nations and elsewhere in the world. For that reason alone, I made sure I gave it the widest circulation. I felt satisfied that the month I had spent at IFPRI achieved its intended purpose.

Finally, I never lost sight of the significance of participating in international conferences whenever the subject under discussion was within my sphere of competence. The Executive Director's decision to exclude me altogether from participating in WFC Workshops and Ministerial Conferences had been deliberately done to keep me out of touch with professional colleagues, and I felt the need to do something to repair the damage in that regard. Of course, I would not solicit any invitations to conferences, as I knew well enough that the Executive Director would not grant me permission to attend them. But every now and then, an invitation would come my way unsolicited, sometimes channelled through the Executive Director, and sometimes directly. In every such case, I would make sure that I presented a powerful case that left him no choice but to grant his approval.

A case in point was a personal invitation I received in June 1990 to attend a symposium at the Institute of Developing Economies in Tokyo scheduled for December 1990. The Executive Director would certainly have prevented my participation if he could. However, circumstances made it impossible for him to do so. Had the invitation been sent to, or through, the WFC, he could easily have turned it down, or designated someone else to attend. But this particular invitation was unmistakably sent to me in my personal capacity. The invitation read:

"We would like to request your participation in the above symposium and ask that you present a paper ... We are convinced that your participation will enrich and broaden the whole proceedings ... We hope that you

> *would take up the subject of 'Problems of Food Marketing in Tanzania ... Implications for Food Security'*

> *"In the event you agree to participate, IDE will provide you with an honorarium for the paper ... as well as round-trip air transportation, and accommodation in Tokyo"*

As it turned out, the subject of the paper was exactly the thesis of the doctoral dissertation I had presented at the Food Research Institute in Stanford University some 15 years before (This had later appeared as a book by a New York publisher).

On 5 July 1990, I sent the Executive Director a cable, seeking his permission to attend the symposium. It read:

> *"Please find attached copy of a letter I have just received from the Institute of Developing Economies in Tokyo inviting me to present a paper on 'Problems of Staple Food Marketing in Tanzania – Implications for Food Security' at a symposium to be held in Tokyo ... My participation will be in an individual capacity and at no cost to the United Nations.*

> *"I request your kind permission for me to accept this invitation"*

It is a measure of his reluctance to grant the request that it took the Executive Director a full month before he would respond. Eventually, on 9 August 1990, came his reply:

> *"Pleased to authorize your participation in Symposium of the Institute of Developing Economies in Tokyo...it being understood that this will be at no cost to the United Nations".*

I regarded this as a major victory – a booster to my professional morale – which I attributed largely to two factors that had, in effect, put the Executive Director in a tight corner: first, the cost to the United Nations was zero, and second, he had not assigned me any work to do. This made it impossible for him to deny me authorization on any pretext whatsoever.

As he half-heartedly granted the authorization, he stipulated, "I would wish to see a copy of your presentation before it is given". Now, I do not normally disregard instructions from my superiors. But this one was one too many, and I treated it with the contempt it deserved.

But, though I would not submit my paper to the Executive Director for his *approval*, I did circulate it to a number of professional colleagues, including Goran Ohlin, John Mellor, Cristian Ossa, Gerry Helleiner, and the Executive Director himself, for any comments they might have.

I then proceeded straight to Tokyo to present the paper. In Tokyo, I mingled with professional colleagues from all corners of the world. My paper was very well received, and was published by the institute, along with others, in book form the following year.

I must confess that the occasion gave me rare satisfaction. The Japanese Institute of Developing Economies had decided to stage this international symposium to celebrate its 30th anniversary, its chosen theme being "Developing Strategies for the 21st Century". The subject could not have been more topical. The symposium attracted scores of participants, mostly university professors and development economists from around the globe. During the three days (December 10-12, 1990) covered by the symposium, a total of 37 papers were presented by invited participants, of whom I was proud to be one.

Not long afterwards, I attended another high-profile meeting, "The International Development Conference". This took place in Washington DC from January 23-25, 1991. I participated in it purely in my personal capacity as a life member of the Society for International Development, which was the organiser of the conference. The theme of the conference was "From Cold War to Cooperation: Dynamics of a New World Order".

I particularly valued the opportunity to brush shoulders with several senior U.N. officials, many of whom already knew and sympathised with my plight. Though this was not a U.N-sponsored meeting, it was noted for the presence of several prominent U.N. officials. For instance, the Administrator of the UNDP, Mr William H. Draper III, was among four eminent speakers in the two-hour opening plenary, which was chaired by Canadian Ambassador Stephen Lewis; while Mr Goran Ohlin, U.N. Assistant Secretary-General, Department of International Economic and Social Affairs, was the moderator of the Panel on "Trade Policies to help the Poorer Countries".

All in all, I must say that my activities throughout the year 1990, and 1991, elevated me, as I had hoped and prayed, to a level which gave me peace of mind, boosted my self-confidence and gave me courage to face the future. With the ground so well prepared, I now felt ready to tackle the Executive Director of the World Food Council, and indeed the U.N. Administration, head-on.

CHAPTER XI

MY APPEAL TO THE JOINT APPEALS BOARD

"...if I must die, I will die in action, fighting. I will not lie down and close my eyes to be butchered".

(i) The Prelude

First, let me say that from the day I received the Executive Director's letter of 12 June 1989 telling me to "consider looking around in New York (or elsewhere) for another post by the end of the year", I made it clear that I was going to fight it out to the finish. Whether or not my resolve was taken seriously, I do not know. In my first 'interim reply' dated 18 July 1989, I politely appealed to the Executive Director to recognise that the WFC Liaison Office under my leadership had done a good job. I told him that "The idea of my leaving the Council at the end of the year is something that I cannot seriously entertain ... and I crave your understanding not to pursue it".

On 21 July 1989, I wrote one of my first letters to Mr Kofi Annan, Under-Secretary General, Office of Human Resources, complaining bitterly about Mr Trant's unfounded criticisms of me, stating that my performance track record over the past 12 years since I joined the United Nations had been judged outstanding by everyone, including Mr. Trant himself, prior to this moment.

I ended my letter saying: "I do not believe the United Nations will agree to dispose of me so easily, and, win or lose, I intend to use the established staff machinery to the last". Again, whether or not Mr. Annan took me seriously I cannot say.

However, the next two letters I received from Mr. Annan dispelled any doubt as to where the Administration stood on the issue. The first letter, dated 6 September 1989 informed me, without stating any reason, that I was "on a transitional post slated to be abolished by 31 December 1989". On 22 September, I wrote to Mr Annan to say that "the decision of the Executive Director of the World Food Council is unjust, discriminatory, and taken in bad faith.... His decision is therefore unacceptable to me. Please treat this letter as my notice to you of my intention to contest his decision" (See Annex 1.6)

The next letter from Mr Annan, dated 7 December, repeated the same message. It referred to the on-going staff reduction exercise, how some staff had been placed on core posts which were securely funded, while others, including myself, were " encumbering a non-core post, that is, a post scheduled to be abolished by the end of 1989"

By now it was clear to me that the Administration, on which I had pinned hopes to restrain Mr. Trant from expelling me from the Council, had in fact sided with him and endorsed his decision, and was already in process of implementing it. Time was not on my side. The 31st December deadline for me to quit the Council was only a couple of weeks away. What was I to do?

Fortunately, I was in close touch with my counsel, Mr Thomas Dube, a tough lawyer and fellow U.N. employee from Zimbabwe, who was known for his ability and willingness to defend staff interests. On his advice, I ensured that I followed meticulously all the formalities – such as, giving notices, observing deadlines, etc. – for making an appeal to the Joint Appeals Board. I did not want to see my case thrown out for failure to fulfil some procedural technicality.

The 31ˢᵗ December, 1989 came and went uneventfully. I no longer harboured any fear of being dismissed at a time when I was in the thick of a fight to stay on. On 21 February 1990, I wrote my final letter to Mr Kofi Annan in which I challenged the legality of the actions that Mr. Trant had taken against me during my absence on home leave in order to prepare the ground for my dismissal. These took the form of what in the U.N. are called 'P.5 personnel actions' – procedural administrative steps which enabled him to take my core post away from me, assign it to another staff member, and place me on a non-core post slated to be abolished. I wanted to know the reasons for Mr. Trant's actions, and why the Administration, led by Mr Annan, had endorsed them.

Knowing this would probably be my last letter to the Administration before submitting my case to the Joint Appeals Panel, my 3-page letter was as emotional as it was hard-hitting. In the penultimate paragraph, I minced no words:

"Dear Mr Annan, I submit to you that I am the victim of an illegal act, intentionally designed and perpetrated to kill my career, for no better reason than that I am standing in somebody's way. I am not just crying for a job and a salary. Something much higher is at stake – a cry for justice. I beseech you, as the highest official ultimately responsible to the Secretary-General for my welfare as a worker in this organization, to protect me. But if I must die, I will die in action, fighting. I will not lie down and close my eyes to be butchered"(See Annex 1.9).

At this late hour, I no longer expected any positive action from the Administration. Matters had already gone too far. Mine had become one of those cases in which a boss, even if he believes he made the wrong decision, sticks to it anyway, at the expense of his victim, for the sake of appearing firm and unwavering as a boss.

I now had no choice but to appeal to the Joint Appeals Board.

(ii). Keeping my legal counsel informed and sensitized

Good stories are interesting to tell, and interesting to read. Be it fiction or non-fiction, any interesting narrative begs the same basic question, why do the characters involved behave the way they do? Is there a moral to their story?

Questions of this kind occurred to me at every turn in the course of my story. Why did my employer or, more exactly, my Executive Director, do what he did? Why did the Administration, under Mr. Annan, support him? Is there any lesson that **bosses** – secretaries-general, managing directors, executive directors, call them by any name – can learn from this unfortunate experience? And is there anything that my fellow workers – the **underdogs** – in the United Nations, and elsewhere, can learn from *my* experience?

Reproduced below are three memos which I sent to my legal counsel, Mr. Thomas Dube, during the crisis. I wrote them in order to make him better acquainted with my circumstances, and keep him properly sensitized about the case as it evolved. Unlike my main narrative – which is a factual account of who did what, where and when – these three particular memos contain information about my own background, as well as my personal views and suspicions as to what may have led my bosses to treat me the way they did.

There were three of these memos. The first was written at the time the JAB appeal was being launched, the second after the Secretary-General had accepted the JAB's recommendations in my favour, and ordered that they be implemented by the Executive Director; the third, written five months after my return to Rome, aimed at updating Mr. Dube on the latest events.

These memos were meant for the eyes of Mr. Dube only. For that reason, I wrote them *by hand* and would not hand them to a typist.

<u>Memo # 1 dated 1 March 1991.</u>

"Dear Tom,

I hope you will forgive this handwritten scribble. It is my attempt to convey to you my depth of feeling and sense of injury caused by the shameless mistreatment that Mr. Trant, the Executive Director of the World Food Council, has perpetrated on me.

My worst regret is not that my job is insecure, bad as that may be. That I can stand. It is an injustice that can be cured. Nor am I worried by the possibility of separation from the service. The system can take care of that, and justly. What I can NOT stand, and I am sure cannot be cured, is the humiliation, the career damage and the tarnished public image before my own country – all of which have been inflicted on me by Mr. Trant without any reason, and with complete impunity.

Please let me say a word about my public standing in my own country, because it means so much to me and my future. Prior to joining ECA in September 1977, I held two successive top civil service positions – first as National Planning Controller in the Ministry of Finance and Planning; and second, as Director, Institute of Finance Management, Dar es Salaam. Both were direct appointments by the President of the United Republic of Tanzania. By virtue of these appointments, I was issued with a Tanzanian Diplomatic Passport in July 1976 which I hold to this day, and in addition I was entitled to First Class air travel and other fringe benefits. I do not know the practice in other countries, but in the case of Tanzania possession of a diplomatic passport by anyone other than ministers, and people accredited to diplomatic missions abroad, is a rare and highly coveted honour, reserved to a few privileged top appointees of the President (e.g. Permanent Secretaries, the Chief Justice, etc.). This is the echelon in which I was placed.

In Tanzania, then, a passport is more than just a travel document; it is an important symbol of public recognition. Knowing this, I have always found it a source of personal pride and satisfaction that my country has chosen to allow me to continue holding the diplomatic passport, long after I had left to join the U.N. This says something of the public esteem in which I am still held in Tanzania, where my services are seen both as a credit to the U.N. and to my country. I need hardly say that there are a number of Tanzanians who are senior to me within the U.N. hierarchy, travelling on red U.N. passports, but who do not enjoy the same public recognition at home as I do.

It is therefore not the way I regard myself, but the thought of how others have always regarded me over the years, that has intensified my personal agony and heightened my sense of injury at the manner in which Mr. Trant has insulted and tried to discard me. Human decency apart, he forgets that he is my boss not necessarily because he is better regarded in his home country, Canada, than I am in my home country, Tanzania, but simply because his country happens for the time being to have more political clout than mine. In different circumstances, our roles could easily have been interchanged.

Perhaps I may also say a word about the circumstances of my recruitment and tenure in the U.N. In my country, a Presidential appointee is not expected to seek or accept outside job offers, no matter how attractive. I never sought the ECA post. It was ECA itself which, in August 1977 identified me for a P-5 post in the Economic Co-operation Office for which they thought I was ideally suited. The offer was made through our ambassador in Addis, communicated to our Foreign Ministry in Dar, and cleared directly with the President's Office; and only on receiving formal permission from the President did I agree to accept the ECA post 'on secondment'.

At the end of my first fixed-term contract, ECA was extremely pleased with my performance and requested my government for an extension, which was readily granted. Then came a succession of A-rated performance evaluation reports by the ECA, and later by WFC, followed by my conversion to permanent terms after my promotion to D-1 in January 1984. I recall that many of my colleagues were pleasantly surprised when I was awarded a permanent contract, because they knew that it was the Appointment and Promotion Board's normal practice to award permanent terms of service only to younger staff in the P-3/P-4 cadres, and seldom to older people like myself whose first point of entry to the service was P-5 or higher. Naturally, I saw this as further confirmation of what everyone of my supervisors had openly acknowledged in my performance evaluation reports, where the record was consistently outstanding.

Tom, you know the rest. You know, for example, that I served as Officer-in-Charge of the World Food Council for three months before Mr. Trant arrived, and that he himself was very pleased with what I did, and gave me an A-rated evaluation at the time of my transfer to New York.

As I may have said to you earlier, I believe that three circumstances prepared the altar on which I was sacrificed:

First, Mr. Trant's 4-year term was coming to an end in August 1990. He badly needed an extension – which he has since got- for one more year, in order to qualify for a pension. For this he needed the support of France and the U.S., who are two of WFC's staunchest supporters.

Second, my colleague, Mr. Vidal-Naquet, whom Mr. Trant gave the glorified title of' 'Acting Deputy Executive Director' (although he was my junior by far), happened to be French. Just then, he needed a D-1 post to get his promotion implemented.

Third, my immediate subordinate, Ms. Kate Newell, happened to be an American, who had served as Acting Chief of the office before my arrival. She had fought tooth and nail when Mr. Trant tried to transfer her from New York to make room for me, as he had promised me he would. In the end, Mr. Trant yielded and allowed her to remain, but without any redefinition of her functions. Still, she continued to view me as someone standing in her way. At first, Mr. Trant would not pay much attention to her. Then, however, came the time when Mr. Trant suddenly found he needed her support!

You have only to piece the puzzle together to see how all this set the stage for my destruction. The odds against me could not have been stacked higher, and things could not have been cosier for the emerging 'coalition' that was Mr. Trant, Mr.Vidal-Naquet and Ms. Kate Newell. While each of them had his or her own axe to grind, they all shared a common purpose in booting me out of the U.N., not necessarily because they hated me but because it served their interests.

Picture it for yourself. By taking away my post, Mr. Trant could solve all his problems at once. Mr. Vidal-Naquet would have his D-1, Ms. Kate Newell would be re-installed, to her delight, in her previous position as Acting Chief, and – now that their nationals had been appeased – the support of both France and the United States for the extension of Mr. Trant's contract would be assured.

Apparently, Mr.Trant calculated, not entirely mistakenly, that the risk he would be taking by victimizing me would be relatively small. For one thing, my country, Tanzania, had no political clout. It was not even a member of the World Food Council. For another, the timing was particularly opportune in that there was already an on-going mandatory staff reduction exercise within the U.N., and Mr. Trant could always claim – as indeed he did – that he was laying me off for reasons of economy or redundancy. The only thing he forgot was that even in cases of redundancy, the U.N. had laid down a clear-cut procedure to be followed by programme managers in order to protect staff members from precisely the kind of victimization to which he wanted to subject me. Either Mr. Trant was ignorant of this procedure, or else, in his characteristic arrogance, he may have felt that being an Assistant Secretary-General and an Executive Director, he could simply ignore it and get away with it. And so far indeed he has. It remains to be seen whether he will now be taken to task for it, or whether the Joint Appeals Board will look the other way.

This is my fifty-fifth year. If I had remained in the Tanzanian civil service, I would have retired this year, at 55, which is the compulsory retirement age there. Those of my colleagues who knew me in the system assume that I shall retire honourably from the U.N. five years from now. Everyone (including myself) thinks I am lucky, and I have personally worked hard and conscientiously throughout my career in the U.N. to live up to the faith that others have in me. This thought used to inspire me. But now the same thought drives me crazy the moment I remember how Mr. Trant has tried to destroy me.

For two years since my 'crisis' began, I have lived in a nightmare. From respected ones in my own country, to my U.N. colleagues, to those I meet in the corridors, to my own children at home – everyone is asking the same incredulous question, "But, Peter, what have you done?" I wish to repeat the same question to the Secretary-General: "What have I done?"

I have three dependent children, one in college, and two in high school. Apart from the anguish to me, Mr. Trant has no right subjecting me and my family to this kind of anxiety and stress of job insecurity and future uncertainty. I hope I shall be justly compensated for this mental torture."

Memo # 2 dated 10 September 1991.
"Dear Tom,

The time has certainly arrived to take my case to the Tribunal. It seems to be the ideal moment. Trant's foot-dragging, his reluctance to act or talk, and his refusal to implement the Secretary-General's directive – all in order to continue humiliating me – can no longer be tolerated. This man thinks we are all fools. He dare not reject the Secretary-General's instruction flatly, because he knows that would spell the end of his own U.N. career. Therefore he is 'implementing' it on his own terms, at his own pace. This is what we cannot permit.

I now gather that he has begun to flirt with his own countryman, Dick Foran, to upgrade a P-5 post for me, a manoeuvre we have already pre-empted by our (as yet unanswered) letter to the Secretary-General. I believe Trant derives some comfort from the knowledge that Ahtisaari is not coming back. He may also be feeling slightly upbeat now that his own contract, I hear, has been extended for another year.

But none of this can intimidate us!

As regards the actual substance of the appeal to the Tribunal, I think our strategy should be to have the smallest number of points, or counts, which are absolutely unassailable, and which can attract a favourable verdict quickly. We shall strike where it hurts most. We shall hit below the belt. Fortunately, we already know, from experience, Trant's Achille's heel – namely, his contemptuous attitude, his refusal to reply, his couldn't –care-less attitude. We could, and should, now turn his weakness to our advantage.

We do so by picking those counts which are not only unassailable (because they are palpably true), but which can also be couched in a manner that offends the ego of this 'important' man. I know you can do this skilfully within accepted limits of etiquette and legal norms. There will then be a high probability that he will shrug it off and not reply. Should that happen, he will have damaged himself and played into our own hands.

Even if this scenario doesn't materialize, and Trant were in fact to be prevailed upon by those who know better to at least answer our charges before the Tribunal, we can make those charges so unassailably water-tight that he will not have much of a chance.

Such are my layman's views as to strategy and tactics. Consonant with these, I'd propose the following counts:

1. Trant's illegal seizure of my post, and his refusal to restore it despite the JAB's unanimous finding and the Secretary-General's instruction. He has no defence at all here. Our victory is complete.

2. Trant's refusal to assign me any work in the Council, not only <u>before</u> the Secretary-General's directive, but particularly <u>after.</u> Two Council Ministerial sessions have come and gone without my participation. Trant has kept me on the shelf, in 'cold storage', for two full years. The last session in Denmark came two months <u>after</u> he had been ordered to restore me to

my post. Yet he didn't budge. He still excluded me. Against this, consider how much I am costing the U.N.

3. Trant's conduct is deliberately calculated to damage my career, and to make it hard or impossible for me to obtain subsequent employment, whether in the U.N. or elsewhere. This is malice aforethought. We can prove it by what he has written (e.g. writing <u>secretly</u> to the Assistant Secretary-General to say I am operating at P-3 level, while knowing full well what my 12-year performance track record has been, and while knowing that my entry level to the U.N. in 1977 was P-5!). Today I am at D-1 Step 7, the top of the D-1 scale.

4. Trant's conduct is deliberately calculated to humiliate me as a person. This is obvious at a glance. And to me it is what hurts most. And I am sure Trant knows it – and maliciously enjoys it! What must be answered is why the system, why the Secretary-General, tolerates such an injustice when perpetrated by one staff member on another. Is it just because the perpetrator happens to be the supervisor?

To prove our case, three unassailable examples can be quoted. I cite the first two rhetorically:

(a) Who else, or where else in the entire U.N. system, has a D-1/7 been known to work under a girl at P-4-turned-P-5?

(b) Where else, in the entire history of administration and management, in theory let alone in practice, is there a case that is more humiliating and degrading than one in which a supervisor is forced to work in his old office, under the supervision of the same subordinate whom he had been supervising and whom he had on several occasions tried to discipline? This is the exact scenario of my present position vis a vis Ms. Newell.

(c) The secret defamatory letter from Trant to the Assistant Secretary-General, Human Resources Management, already cited, is another clear example of personal humiliation.

<u>The remedy sought.</u>

Against these counts, my re-absorption or rehabilitation in the World Food Council or elsewhere in the U.N., even if it occurs, is clearly an inadequate redress of my grievances.

I have been subjected to torture and humiliation, to mental anguish, anxiety and job insecurity. I have lost face and esteem in the eyes of my compatriots, and before my government, which always held me in high esteem, to the extent that I still hold a diplomatic passport as a public symbol of that recognition.

The damage that Trant has done to my image is irreparable and irreversible; and this without the slightest excuse on his part.

No, Tom, we sure can't let them get away with this. The Administrative Tribunal ought to award me a <u>sizeable cash compensation.</u> My appeal is not for a job – after all I still have a job and a salary – my appeal is for <u>just compensation,</u> commensurate with the damage caused to me.

Sincerely yours,
Peter"

<u>Memo # 3 dated 3 April 1992.</u>

"Dear Tom,

Sorry it took this long to send you this 'continuation of my story'. The fight isn't over but it's more subtle, and low-keyed, but just as vicious. Chances are Trant departs June 30, but who ever knows?

Just now we are preparing for our Nairobi session to be held at the end of June.

You get a quick and accurate perspective if you read this in the sequence as numbered.

1. Trant half-heartedly welcomes me to Rome, while announcing to the world that I am not a 'perfect match' for the post.

2. UNDP, New York, want to send me out on what would have been a high-profile mission for me, shortly before my return to Rome. On receiving this request, Trant is green with envy, and decides he will stop it at all costs.

3. In this letter Trant tries to find lame excuses for saying 'no' – pretends that I ought to be busy enough in New York and/or with preparations for my departure to Rome. This hypocritical posture naturally infuriates me.

4. I lash out at Trant and expose his hypocrisy. As expected, he badly resents this.

5. Trant is furious, and slams the door shut to any further talking, either to me or to UNDP, to whom:

6. He writes separately. Goes so far as to pretend that Mr. Uwe Kracht (my German colleague) should have been the man to contact, and not Peter Temu.

7. At last I consider the time ripe for me to answer his insulting invitation to return to Rome, while at the same time accepting the invitation.

8. Seeing that Trant was reluctant to introduce me to anyone, I draft a letter of self-introduction, and get him to sign and circulate it to U.N. agencies and Headquarter's Departments. A similar letter is sent to World Food Council member states.

9. First formal written clash with Trant since my arrival in Rome.(N.B. Anne Rogers was Officer-in-Charge of my Unit prior to my appointment here, and had been slated to take over. Hates my guts! Something of a replay of my New York Liaison Office case – a replay I have publicly stated I will not tolerate.

10. Trant hits back, rebukes me, slights me, and showers praise on Anne Rogers.

11. Tension between me and Anne Rogers grows, stemming from her refusal to report to me but always to Trant, before whom she undermines my work.

12. Trant angrily decides, with my concurrence, that Anne Rogers will henceforth report to him directly, withdraws her from my Section, and substitutes Borissenko.

13. Just one of several memos from my colleagues (the only other D-1) complaining against Anne Rogers and Trant's 'shielding' of her.

Yours ever,
Peter"

(iii) The Appeal Procedure

The appeal process in the U.N. is a two-level procedure. First, an aggrieved staff member had to bring his case before the Joint Appeals Board (JAB). Second, if the JAB failed to resolve the matter, an appeal would then be made to the U.N. Administrative Tribunal, the 'highest court of appeal', whose decisions are final and binding on the Secretary-General and on the staff member alike.

The JAB, as set up to hear my case, was made up of a four-member panel, whose chairman was appointed by the Secretary-General. According to the established procedure, the JAB panel would hear the case from the appellant, as well as the response from the Administration. After due deliberation, the JAB would pronounce its verdict in favour of, or against, the staff member, as the case might be. Its findings, usually unanimous, would normally be accompanied by recommendations for remedial action. These findings would then be submitted to the Secretary-General who might accept, or reject, its recommendations at his own discretion.

If accepted by the Secretary-General, the recommendations became binding, and had to be implemented by the Secretariat; but if rejected, they were simply regarded as an input into the organization's decision-making process, leaving the staff member free to appeal to the Administrative Tribunal if he so wished.

Even as I was preparing my case for the JAB, the Executive Director of WFC was resorting to a myriad of administrative manoeuvres in a frantic effort to have his decision implemented. But, contrary to expectations, many of these manoeuvres, far from serving the purpose he intended, unwittingly playing into our hands, giving me and my counsel the legal ammunition we needed to fight back. From the beginning, my correspondence with the Executive Director, and with

Mr. Kofi Annan, had left no doubt that I was going to put up a tough fight, but this only added to the Executive Director's eagerness to be rid of me soonest.

Unfortunately for him, his condescending attitude towards me and towards lower-ranking but responsible officials in the Secretariat, cost him dearly. For example, he would not respond to queries addressed to him by responsible officials in the Administration. Probably, his worst single blunder was his refusal to respond at all to my formal *Appeal to the Joint Appeals Board* submitted on 29 June 1990. This fact was duly noted in a four-word paragraph of the JAB report, which simply states: "Respondent has not replied".

The Executive Director took at least two administrative actions – both in vain – in trying to get me ousted. First, during my absence on home leave, and taking advantage of a staff retrenchment exercise which was then in progress, he sneakily took away my regular (or 'core') post, gave it to another staff member, and assigned me a 'non-core' post slated to be abolished on 31 December 1989. To my dismay, the Office of Human Resources Management under Mr. Kofi Annan endorsed his action, but its implementation failed, because I successfully challenged it on procedural grounds.

Second, the Executive Director submitted an official Performance Evaluation Report of my work which, if accepted, would have been the worst in the entire history of my U.N. career. Unfortunately for him, he overplayed his hand: the 'evaluation' was so full of smears and inconsistencies that it totally undermined his own credibility as a responsible supervisor. I was quick to expose the slurs and slanders in a strongly worded rebuttal, in which I pointed out, among other things, that the so-called 'performance evaluation' was malicious: it had been done retroactively, and was "suitably tailored to justify the damage he had already done". Consequently, the Executive Director's purported evaluation of my performance never became part of the official record. .

This was a fight to the finish. Once started, there was no looking back. The reader, and certainly my contemporaries and successors in the United Nations, are entitled to know the truth of what actually happened. And the best way to do them – and myself – justice is to lay bare the verbatim record of what happened.

(iv) The submission by my legal counsel, Mr. Thomas Dube: actual record

"Appeal to the Joint Appeals Board
Submitted on 29 June 1990
Appellant; Peter E. Temu, World Food Council

(a) Submission for administrative review.

1. A request for a review of the administrative decision that is the subject of the present appeal was submitted to the Secretary-General in compliance with Staff Rule 111.2 on 2 March 1990. Its receipt was acknowledged by Ms Diana Boernstein, Chief of the Administrative Review Unit, on 6 April 1990. She informed the appellant that the Secretary-General would reply within a month of the date of her letter, failing which he could appeal to the Joint Appeals Board within the month following.

2. The period during which the Secretary-General should have replied expired uneventfully on 6 May 1990. The appellant had to submit his appeal to the Joint Appeals Board before 6 June 1990. On being requested by the appellant, the Presiding

Officer of the Joint Appeals Board allowed an extension of the deadline to 30 June 1990.

(b) Description of the contested action which violated the appellant's terms of service

3. The administrative decision which the appellant is contesting is the decision by the Executive Director of the World Food Council to deprive him of his established D-1 post, number UNT-01018-E-D-1-002. This is the post against which the appellant was recruited to the Council on 1 January 1984 and which he has encumbered ever since, first in Rome and now in New York. The post has never been abolished. Nor has it ever been taken away from the Council to be deployed elsewhere. It has simply been taken away from the appellant for the benefit of his colleague, Mr. Alain Vidal-Naquet.

4. Until now, Mr. Vidal-Naquet has encumbered a D-2 post, number UNT-01018-E- D-2-001, against which he was promoted on 1 October 1986 [see Document 3]. This post was dis-established and became supernumerary on 31 December 1989. Thus its incumbent found himself without a secure post. By switching that post to the appellant, in exchange for the appellant's own post which is funded and secure, the Executive Director has succeeded in reversing the positions – the career fortunes – of these two staff members, Mr. Vidal-Naquet and Mr. Temu, in favour of the former and at the expense of the latter.

5. This enforced swapping of posts, formalised through P.5 actions submitted by the Executive Director on the 21 December 1989 under cover of his Executive Officer's letter dated 20 January

1990 completes the administrative action which is the subject of the present appeal.

6. Despite the pain and anguish that this decision has caused to the appellant, at no time has the administration cared to explain the reasons for its action, even when specifically requested to do so. Instead, for having dared to demand an explanation, the appellant has been punished by the Executive Director, who has tried to isolate him by cutting him off from the main stream of the Council's activities for more than a year.

The date of the disputed decision and the injury it has caused to the appellant.

7. Strictly, the date of the disputed decision is 21 December 1989, [Document 4], a date conveniently chosen by the Executive Director to coincide with the appellant's absence on home leave. On that day, the administrative P.5 action was filed. For book-keeping convenience, the decision was regularised on 9 April 1990, cleared by the Office of Human Resources Management on 11 May 1990, and its effective date backdated to 1 January 1990. It should also be noted that earlier, through his letter dated 28 July 1989, the Executive Director had tried in vain to impose the decision, and was prevented by the Office of Human Resources Management.

8. The injury the decision has caused to the appellant is obvious. First, the appellant has been treated unjustly, contrary to his terms of service and the accepted norms of the Organization. He has been oppressed and discriminated against. Second, after serving his country and the United Nations for many years with distinction, the appellant, at age 53, has suddenly

been thrown into a state of confusion and uncertainty, and put in jeopardy, from the point of view of his job security and career benefits for himself and his family. Third, the appellant's hitherto well-respected professional image before his colleagues, before the public and in the eyes of his own country, has been tarnished, if not shattered, by an employer eager to discredit him and portray him as a failure in order to disguise his baseless discriminatory actions.

9. The appellant's sense of injury has been heightened by recollections of a number of acts of omission and commission by the Executive Director aimed not only at ensuring that he does not retain his present job but that he will face maximum difficulty getting employment elsewhere. A clear example of an act of omission has been the Executive Director's refusal to comply with the Administrative Instruction ST/AI/353 because he knew that if he had done so, the appellant, as the most senior of the D-1 staff, would have had an edge over the other staff in the same category and certainly could not have been singled out for elimination.

10. As an act of commission one may refer to the particularly cynical incident, in which the Executive Director, having made up his mind that he wanted the appellant out of the Council, wrote to the Assistant Secretary-General/Office of Human Resources Management to ask him to find the appellant an alternative job, while also insinuating that he was really unfit for any job. His letter of 13 June 1989 states, "Temu is operating at a level closer to a P-3 rather than a D-1". To anyone who understands the difference between D-1 and P-3 this message, apart from its underlying insult, simply meant that the appellant was

unfit for any responsible job. It particularly hurts to think that such a letter was never copied to the appellant himself. The Executive Director decided to send it to Mr. Kofi Annan, in non-confidential cover, so that anyone else in the Secretariat would see it, but not Mr. Temu himself. For an officer who was Chief of an office, this backbiting was a humiliation of the worst kind.

(d) The facts, as they evolved.

11. Before the contested decision was finally formalized, the dispute had been simmering for several months, during which the attitude of the Administration oscillated indecisively in a 'go-stop-go' fashion particularly agonizing to the appellant. First came the curt note from the Executive Director dated 28 July 1989 telling the appellant that he had "been determined to be against a transitional post". The crude language of this short, sharp note surprised the appellant, as did the complete absence of any explanation as to why such a decision had been made, by whom, and what it meant for the appellant's career.

12. The next thing the appellant did was approach the Office of Human Resources Management for clarification, seeing first Mr. Annan and then Mr. Riesco. At first he was informed that the Office of Human Resources Management knew nothing about it, and reassured that such a drastic decision could not be imposed by the Executive Director, and in any case could not be legal or binding until endorsed by the Office of Human Resources Management. The appellant was further told that the Office of Human Resources Management would seek clarification from the Executive Director and that the

appellant need not, in the meantime, answer the note or take any other action. "Simply ignore it, until you hear from us!", advised Mr. Riesco,

13. There followed a long interval during which the Office of Human Resources Management never called the appellant to brief him on any developments, and the appellant's own efforts to contact anyone in the Office of Human Resources Management were unsuccessful. Then the appellant received a letter dated 6 September 1989 signed by the Assistant Secretary-General/Office of Human Resources Management, Mr. Kofi Annan, which stated, among other things, that the appellant had been placed on a transitional post slated to be abolished on 31 December 1989. Through that letter the appellant also learned, for the first time, that the decision had been reached in accordance with Administrative Instruction ST/AT/353 of 18 July 1988 entitled "Internal Re-assignment of Staff: Guidelines for <u>ad hoc</u> Joint Departmental Panels" [Document 10]. The same point was to be repeated in a subsequent letter from the Office of Human Resources Management to the appellant, again signed by Mr. Annan, dated 7 December 1989 which stated, in part, that "Staff members on non-core posts were generally identified by departmental retrenchment panels on the basis of the criteria set out in Administrative Instruction ST/AI/353".

14. As the situation continued to unfold, the appellant's confusion and astonishment grew. In particular, on studying the contents of ST/AI/353 he noted that the Administrative Instruction included the following provision: "In order to ensure that staff re-assignments are undertaken in a fair and objective

manner, the Secretary-General has decided that <u>ad hoc</u> joint departmental panels <u>shall</u> be established to advise heads of departments and offices on the internal re-assignment of their staff". This makes it clear that the decision was mandatory, not discretional.

15. One thing is crystal clear. The Executive Director of the World Food Council has never appointed an <u>ad hoc</u> joint departmental panel to advise him on retrenchment or internal re-assignment of his staff. Instead of complying, as required, with the Secretary-General's Administrative Instruction, which would have protected the rights of the appellant, the Executive Director deliberately chose to disregard it, to the detriment of the appellant. This is not a case of a staff member being denied a core post and put on a non-core post for reasons of retrenchment or re-assignment. It is a case of a staff member being deprived of a core post and put on a non-core post for unknown reasons, or for no reasons at all beyond the fact such a procedure makes it easy for the Executive Director to take the next step, that is, to expel him from the Organization.

16. Two questions arise. First, if proper reasons exist for the action taken, why has the applicant been denied the right to know them? Second, why does the Assistant Secretary-General/ Human Resources Management claim, not once but twice, that Administrative Instruction ST/AI/353 has been followed, although it is obvious that it has not?

17. It is for these reasons that on 22 September 1989 the appellant formally notified the Assistant Secretary-General/Office of Human Resources Management, Mr. Kofi Annan, that he

could not accept the decision of the Executive Director and that he would have to appeal against it.

18. At this juncture there was renewed activity in the form of further direct contacts between the appellant, the Assistant Secretary-General/Office of Human Resource Management and the Executive Director in an effort to reach a settlement. These contacts, which were always cordial and seemingly reassuring, raised the appellant's hopes and led him to believe, or deceived him into believing, that the decision to take away his post would be rescinded. There were indications that the Office of Human Resources Management was probably urging the Executive Director of WFC to change his mind.

19. For a while, these efforts appeared to bear fruit. On 19 October 1989, the Executive Director in a letter copied to the appellant, informed the Assistant Secretary-General/Office of Human Resources Management that after discussions with the appellant, he had agreed that "with changed responsibilities" the appellant could "make a useful and important contribution to the Council". This was confirmed in subsequent correspondence between the Executive Director and the appellant, culminating in the Executive Director's letter dated 10 January 1990 in which he spells out the terms of reference of the appellant's new responsibilities as the Council's Senior Policy Advisor.

20. At that point, it seemed to the appellant that his fears had been allayed, that the Administration had begun to demonstrate its good faith, and there was no longer much cause for alarm. He little suspected that this was only the calm before the storm.

21. For the appellant soon learned that during his absence on home leave, and unknown to him, the Executive Director had signed

an administrative P.5 action on 29 December 1989 swapping his post with Mr. Vidal-Naquet's. Even on his return from home leave and after he had discussions with the Executive Director, the appellant was still kept in the dark about the action that the Executive Director had taken. Indeed the very letter concerning the P.5 action which was sent to the appellant's office on 20 January 1990 after his return from home leave, was addressed not to him but to his deputy, who quietly tucked it away. It was just by accident that the appellant happened to bump into a copy of that letter in his personnel file to discover that it had been written almost a month before!

22. The appellant felt cheated, his faith betrayed. He therefore set in motion the appeal process with his letter of 21 February 1990 to the Assistant Secretary-General/Office of Human Resources Management requesting an administrative review of the decision to take his post away.

(e) The remedy requested

23. The appellant recognizes full well and deeply regrets that the damage done to his professional image by the Executive Director could be permanent and irreparable. There is no way the harm can be fully remedied. The appellant can only request that the Administration desist from aggravating the injury and injustice already perpetrated.

24. The appellant hopes, at least, that the Joint Appeals Board will prevail on the Secretary-General to return the appellant's post to him unconditionally, in recognition of his status as a permanent international civil servant in good standing who, in the words of his own Executive Director, "can make an

important contribution to the Council". The appellant should immediately be removed from the supernumerary staff pool and the insecurity that goes with it.

25. In parenthesis, it may be relevant to inform the members of the Joint Appeals Board that since the launching of this appeal, Mr Alain Vidal-Naquet, the chosen beneficiary of the appellant's post, has resigned, leaving the post vacant. In a recent cable to him from the United Nations Director of the Budget, the Executive Director has been specifically informed that "once vacated, a retrenchment post may not be encumbered" and that "authorized posts must remain blocked as long as supernumeraries continue". Despite his protests, the appellant is as of this moment still regarded as a supernumerary. The fact that a post (coincidentally the appellant's own post) is now open, is a further reason why the appellant's rightful post should now be returned to him".

It is noteworthy that once the Joint Appeals Board got down to business, it went about its task most expeditiously. I am surprised to this day that the Panel accomplished its work without ever summoning me, or my counsel, for interrogation. Whether the Panel ever summoned Mr Kofi Annan or some other top brass in the U.N. Administration, I do not know. What I do know is that the Executive Director never appeared before the Panel: either he was not summoned or, if he was, he simply refused to show up. He probably may have brushed it all aside, seeing that he was in Rome while the Panel was sitting in New York, working on what to him seemed a routine chore. There was certainly some exchange of written communications, though it would appear from the Panel's report that the Executive Director ignored these too – ultimately to his own detriment.

CHAPTER XII

THE FINDINGS AND RECOMMENDATIONS OF THE JOINT APPEALS BOARD: ACTUAL RECORD

"The Panel, therefore, unanimously recommends that the Appellant be restored to a D-1 post in the World Food Council..."

On 26 March 1991, the findings and recommendations of the JAB were reported to the Secretary-General. Here is the full text:

"CONFIDENTIAL

Report No. 820

Case No. 90-43

26 March 1991

UNITED NATIONS JOINT APPEALS BOARD

REPORT TO THE SECRETAY-GENERAL

Case of Mr Peter Temu

1. The Panel of the Joint Appeals Board composed of Mr. D. Koon, Chairperson, Mr. W. Fuerst, Member appointed by the Secretary-General, and Mr. M. Al-Ali, Member elected by the staff, having considered the appeal lodged by Mr. Peter Temu (hereinafter the Appellant) against the decision to remove him from an established post and to place him against a transitional post, hereby submits its report

Summary of the facts.

2. The appellant was recruited to a Senior Economic Affairs Officer (P-5) post in ECA on a two-year fixed term contract in September 1977. His contract was twice extended for two years, and then converted to probationary in September 1983. The overall ratings given him in PERs prepared during his service in ECA were, successively, "a very good performance", "an outstanding performance", and "an outstanding performance". A fourth report covering his final period of service in ECA, but prepared some time after his departure, gave him a rating of "an excellent performance"

3. In 1983, Appellant applied for the post at the D-1 level of Chief, Policy Development and Economic Analysis at the World Food Council (WFC) in Rome, and was transferred to that post effective 1 January 1984. In March 1985, he was granted a permanent appointment with an effective date of 1 June 1984. In December 1985, he was promoted to D-1 level, effective 1 April 1985. During his period of service in Rome, three PERs were prepared; all three gave him the rating "an excellent performance". Two, for the periods1 January – 30 June 1984, and 1 July 1984 – 30 April 1985, were signed by the then Executive Director, Maurice Williams; the third, for the period May 1985 – 31 October 1986, was signed by the current Executive Director, Gerald Trant.

4. In December 1986, Appellant was assigned to the WFC Office in New York as its Chief. There is no PER on his official status file for the period of his service in New York, although the Executive Director, in a cable of 14 December 1988,

recommended no change in his appointment status. There is no record in the file that a five-year review was completed.

5. On 13 June 1989, the Executive Director wrote the Assistant Secretary-General, OHRM, that:

"Mr. Temu has not been successful in representing the Council or the Council's interests. He is operating at a level closely associated to a P-3 rather than a D-1. If it would be possible to find an alternative post for Mr. Temu, it would be most helpful".

On 28 July 1989, the Executive Director informed the Appellant in a personal and confidential letter that he had "been determined to be against a transitional post". In a letter of 6 September 1989, the Assistant Secretary-General, OHRM, told the Appellant, "The Office of Human Resources Management has been informed by WFC, in accordance with Administrative Instruction ST/AI/353 of 18 July 1988 [sic] on the internal reassignment of staff that you are on a transitional post slated to be abolished by 31 December 1989". This was followed by a letter of 7 December 1989 from the same source, which said, <u>inter alia,</u> "...staff members on non-core posts were generally identified by departmental retrenchment panels on the basis of the criteria set out in Administrative Instruction ST/AI/353." On 21 December 1989, a personnel action was signed by the Executive Director, moving the Appellant from the post he had occupied since his transfer from ECA to a post shown as UNT- 01018-X-D-2-001. (This was later amended to UNT-01018-U-D-2-001) to conform with the designation for a post to be provided for a "supernumerary" staff member as per the instructions of the Director of the Budget in a cable dated 13 February 1990)

6. On 21 February 1990, the Appellant wrote to the Assistant Secretary-General, OHRM, claiming that he had learned of

that action only recently and by accident, that it was illegal and that he intended to contest it. On 2 March 1990, he informed the Assistant Secretary-General, OHRM, that he wished his previous letter to be considered a request for administrative review under the terms of Staff Rule 111.2(a). The Chief, Administrative Review Unit, acknowledged receipt in a letter dated 6 April 1990. In a memorandum dated 22 May 1990, the Appellant informed the Presiding Officer of his intent to file An appeal under the terms of Staff Rule 111.2(a)(ii), and requested an Extension to permit him to consult with counsel. He filed his appeal on 29 June 1990.

Summary of contentions

7. Appellant's contentions may be summarized, as follows:

i.   the Executive Director had Appellant moved from his permanent post to a transitional post as a preliminary to his "elimination" from the WFC;

ii. this change in post, taken without recourse to the procedures spelled out in ST/AI/353, Internal Reassignment of Staff: Guidelines for ad hoc Joint Departmental panels, was illegal and should therefore be set aside.

8. Respondent has not replied.

Considerations.

9. The panel noted with regret the absence of both a reply to the Appellant's request for administrative review under the terms of Staff Rule111.2(a), and a respondent's reply to the letter of appeal. The Appellant's statement of the facts was, therefore, undisputed. The panel itself took note of the existence of a vacant D-1 post in the World Food Council. This post is

currently being advertised in Vacancy Announcement No.91-E-WFC-203-RO/RECIRC.

10. Counsel for Appellant had asked to be heard by the Panel. It was able, however, to arrive at a conclusion without requiring his assistance.

11. The Panel considered that, in this case, the Administration had failed in its obligation to provide fair treatment and proper and equitable procedures. The Administration did not complete a PER for Appellant, although one was due precisely (October 1989) when the decisions affecting his career were being made (Mr Trant's letter of 13 June 1989 to Mr. Annan can hardly be considered a substitute for a PER). Tha Administration failed to complete the five-year review of permanent appointment required under Staff Rule 104.3(a)(ii) which would have included an evaluation of his performance, although this, too, was due during the critical period. Finally, the Administration did not observe the procedures established under the terms of ST/AI/353, Internal Reassignment of Staff: Guidelines for <u>ad hoc</u> Joint Departmental Advisory Panels.

Recommendation

The Panel, therefore, unanimously recommends that the Appellant be restored to a D-1 post in the World Food Council. In the event, but only in the event, that all D-1 posts in the World Food Council are encumbered, the Panel unanimously recommends that he be transferred to an established D-1 post elsewhere in the Secretariat, in a manner consistent with the terms of Staff Regulation 4.4.

Report and recommendations adopted unanimously by a Panel of the Joint Appeals Board

Signed by:

D. Koon, Chairperson

W. Fuerst, Member appointed by the Secretary-General

M. S. Al-Ali, Member elected by the Staff

M. A. Schlaff, Secretary of the Panel

26 March 1991

Approved on behalf of the Secretary-General

In accordance with my letter to Mr. Peter Temu dated 1 April 1991.

Signed by: Martti Ahtisaari

Under-Secretary-General for Administration and Management

1 April 1991

The JAB's unanimous verdict was communicated to me by Mr. Martti Ahtisaari, United Nations Under-Secretary-General for Administration and Management, with the following covering letter dated 1 April 1991:

"Dear Mr. Temu,

I enclose herewith a copy of Report No. 820 submitted by the Joint Appeals Board on your appeal.

The Secretary-General has re-examined your case in light of the Board's report. On the basis of the Board's recommendation, he has decided that the D-1 post in the World Food Council, which was circulated in vacancy announcement 91-E-WFC-203-RO, should be blocked until such time as a suitable D-1 post is found for you elsewhere and that, in the meantime, you should be placed against this post. The procedures which had been underway for filling of this post in the World Food Council have therefore been suspended.

The above-mentioned decision of the Secretary-General is 'the final decision on the appeal' mentioned by staff rule 111.2(0). Therefore, any further recourse you might wish to file should be addressed to the Administrative Tribunal.

A copy of the Secretary-General's decision and of the Board's report will be transmitted to the President of the Headquarters Staff Committee unless you indicate to us, within one month, that you do not want it to be so transmitted.

Yours sincerely,
Martti Ahtisaari
Under-Secretary-General
for Administration and Management"

On 17 April 1991, I acknowledged Mr Ahtisaari's letter, with a copy to, among others, my legal Counsel, Mr. Thomas Dube, and the Executive Director, Mr Gerald Trant. The letter said:

"Dear Mr Ahtisaari,

I acknowledge receipt of your letter, Reference 2-6-1 dated 1 April 1991, and would like to express my gratitude to you personally and to all those who heard my appeal for your unsparing efforts to see that justice is done.

While this ugly incident within the World Food Council has tarnished my professional image, and caused permanent damage to my career, the appeal process has vindicated my faith in the United Nations and in the integrity of the Secretary-General.

Yours sincerely,
Peter E. Temu"

CHAPTER XIII

THE EXECUTIVE DIRECTOR TRIES IN VAIN TO DODGE IMPLEMENTATION OF THE SECRETARY-GENERAL'S DIRECTIVE.

"Try as he would, there was no clever trick by which the Executive Director could dodge the implementation of the Secretary-General's directive"

The Secretary-General's decision to restore me to my D-1 post was a great triumph for me and a gross humiliation for the Executive Director. His hostile administrative manoeuvres had backfired. Now he had no choice but to obey, however reluctantly, the Secretary-General's directive.

Try as he would, there was no clever trick by which the Executive Director could dodge the implementation of the Secretary-General's directive. His last resort was procrastination, that is, deliberate foot-dragging in getting anything done. Indeed, it took a full seven months – that is, from April to November – before he would invite me back to Rome to assume my D-1 post, and even then, only after he had been literally bulldozed into doing so.

During this whole period, while I was no longer under anything like the stress and anxiety that befell me before and during the JAB exercise, I remained watchful nevertheless and followed his every move, determined to keep the heat on. Justice delayed is justice denied. My purpose was to ensure that his delaying tactics would not, in the end, amount to *de facto* non-compliance.

No longer on the defensive, I now pursued relentlessly my single-minded objective of returning to WFC headquarters in Rome. I knew there was little the Executive Director could do to stop me. He was at his wits' end: he had run out of excuses – and out of time – and the pressure from all sides to get him to act was at a new high.

Still, the Executive Director tried a few more desperate manoeuvres before he would finally yield. On 30 April 1991 he sent a three-page memo to Mr Martti Ahtisaari complaining bitterly against the decision of the JAB. But whatever merit may have attached to his memo, it was a classic case of 'too little, too late'. A similar exchange of memos, coupled with direct telephone exchanges between him and Mr Ahtisaari's successor, Mr Richard Foran, Acting Under-Secretary-General, Department of Administration and Management, (and incidentally a fellow Canadian national) similarly came to nothing.

The pressure on the Executive Director to re-instate me at WFC headquarters in Rome now proved irresistible, coming as it did from all directions.

From the Administration's side, Mr. Richard Foran wrote to him two letters, in close succession. The first, dated 17 September 1991, ended by affirming that the Secretary-General's decision should be implemented without any further delay. The second, barely a month later, dated 21 August 1991, ended similarly: *"I should appreciate it if you would proceed without delay to place Mr. P. Temu against the vacant D-1 post"*

I myself was now becoming increasingly agitated. For once, on 1 June 1991, I decided to write directly to the Secretary-General, Mr.

Javier Perez de Cuellar, complaining that his directive had not yet been implemented. I added that Mr. Trant was still refusing to give me assignments and would not let me participate in the Council's sessions. To rub it in, I ended this letter, as I had done several others, with the inciteful remark:

"It is a measure of the extent to which things have deterioratedthat I could be out on a pleasure trip to Niagara Falls … at a time when the Council was meeting   in Denmark for its regular session"

It also occurred to me that the time was opportune for some diplomatic pressure to be brought to bear on the Secretary-General, especially in the event that my own letter either did not reach him, or was simply put aside. Concomitantly with my letter, therefore, I approached my country's Permanent Representative to the United Nations, Ambassador Anthony Nyakyi, briefed him fully about the saga, and requested his intervention on my behalf.

The Ambassador, a former college mate, was sympathetic, and decided to send an Aide Memoire to the UN Secretary-General though I cannot say what impact it had.

Meanwhile, my legal Counsel, Mr Thomas Dube, was determined to take the whole matter to the U.N. Administrative Tribunal, the highest court in the system.

On 19 September 1991, Mr. Dube did just that. He sent formal notification to the Executive Secretary of the U.N. Administrative Tribunal, Maria Vicient-Milburn, which read:

"Notification of Intention to Appeal Pursuant to JAB Report No.820

1. Some months ago, the Joint Appeals Board made a factual finding in favour of Mr. Peter Temu, a D-1 staff member

employed by the World Food Council at its Liaison Office in New York.

2   Pursuant to that favourable finding, the Secretary-General agreed to perform the terms of that favourable finding. The World Food Council, on the other hand, continued (and still continues) to stall in regard to the implementation of the Secretary-General's favourable position to reinstate Mr. Temu to his former position.

3   Mr. Temu has requested me to give you notice of his intention to appeal the unconscionable stalling tactics and delays to reinstate him to his prior position. Accordingly, it is the purpose of this memorandum to achieve the objective of your office, recording and registering this notice of intent."

This notification touched a sensitive cord. For, only two days earlier, in his letter to Mr. Trant, Mr. Foran himself had stated, quite pointedly: "The Secretary-General's decision was taken to avoid what would, in all probability, have been a damaging loss in the Tribunal"(See Annex 6.2). This was an admission that the last thing the Administration wanted to see was an appeal to the U.N. Administrative Tribunal. Mr. Dube's letter of intention to appeal to the Administrative Tribunal had come in the nick of time, and hit the Administration like a hammer. That was the last straw.

On 20 September 1991, Mr. Trant yielded.

In a brief memo to Mr. Foran, he stated; "As you can see from the attachments, action is being taken on Mr. Temu for his return to Rome..." And on that same date, he wrote to me: "Please see my memo to Mr. Ciss. Welcome back to Rome."

I was neither impressed nor excited. I took my time, and exactly three weeks later, on 10 October 1991, I replied:

"I acknowledge with thanks receipt of your letter dated 20 September 1991 inviting me to take up new responsibilities in Rome as Chief, Policy Co-ordination and External Relations.

I welcome an opportunity when we can all put the past behind us, and pull together in the interests of the Council."

Thus ended a relentless struggle, a major drama in my life, that involved many players, *fortunately with a happy ending for me!* My eternal gratitude goes to the top decision makers in the United Nations Secretariat, particularly the Under-Secretary-General, Mr. Martti Ahtisaari (and his successor, Mr.Richard Foran) for seeing to it that justice was done. As stated in my letter to Mr. Martti Ahtisaari, the entire episode, regrettable as it was, ultimately "vindicated my faith in the United Nations, and in the integrity of the Secretary-General".

CHAPTER XIV

PARTNERSHIP BETWEEN WFC AND UNDP COMPROMISED.

It may be worth recalling that another indirect pressure that caused the Executive Director to return me to Rome at the time he did, came from the UNDP in New York. The links I had forged with the UNDP and similar organizations were already beginning to bear fruit, putting me in the limelight, and giving me more professional visibility than the Executive Director would have wished. He therefore tried to cut me off from those links, while at the same time claiming that the Council itself still retained them.

A case in point was the UNDP/WFC informal partnership in the execution of a South-South co-operation project on food security which he totally undermined.

A letter from Mr. Basem Khader, Officer-in-Charge of the UNDP Regional Bureau for Africa, pleaded in vain with Mr. Trant to allow me three weeks in pursuit of this project. Unfortunately, not knowing Mr. Trant's sensitivities, Mr. Khader made the 'mistake' of remarking: "We can think of no one more qualified than Mr. Temu to take up this challenging task". Was he praising me? This was the last thing the Executive Director liked to hear. Summarily, he dismissed Mr. Khader's request, the convenient pretext being that I would not be able to report to Rome in time if I were to undertake the UNDP assignment.

Then, turning to me, the Executive Director gave me a piece of his mind. "I would like you to report to Rome without further delay. If you can make yourself available before 1 November 1991, all the better"(See Annex 3.3)

In fact, the UNDP needed my services for only three weeks, and their request had come exactly three weeks to the date I would be reporting for duty in Rome. Given that the Executive Director had not assigned me any role in the on-going session of the General Assembly, the timing would have suited me, the UNDP, and the WFC perfectly well. But the response from the Executive Director both to the UNDP and to myself was so decisively negative that the whole idea had to be dropped.

In clear demonstration of his resentment at my having been identified by the UNDP, the Executive Director ended his reply to Mr. Khader by informing him that he had assigned the responsibility for the follow-up to Mr. Uwe Kracht, Chief of Policy Development and Economic Analysis, and that he should feel free to contact him any time in connection with the project.

Apparently, this was not the first time the Executive Director had undermined WFC's role in its co-operation with UNDP in the execution of this project. About a year before my services were requested, my colleague, Mr. Alain Vidal-Naquet, the 'Acting Deputy Executive Director', had been appointed overall Co-ordinator of the Project. It had been UNDP's intention that he would continue to play this role, with WFC's support, even after he left the Council in September 1990.

Unfortunately, Mr. Vidal-Naquet resigned as Project Co-ordinator amidst bitter recrimination against the Executive Director (now his former boss). In his widely-circulated letter of resignation, dated 14 December 1990, he stated that his decision had been prompted by the continuing obstructionist and petty attitude of the World Food Council Executive Director, whose present hostile attitude surprisingly contradicted his past attitude towards him when he was still a staff member of the World Food Council. This confession is ample proof that there was no love lost between the Executive Director and his one time 'Acting Deputy'.

It came as no surprise then, that with Mr. Vidal-Naquet out of the way, and myself obviously unacceptable to Mr. Trant, the only remaining senior official who could continue to maintain a formal link with UNDP was the Chief of Policy Development and Economic Analysis, Mr. Uwe Kracht, and Mr. Khader was informed accordingly.

As one might have expected, the 'co-operation' between UNDP and WFC, under Mr. Kracht, suffered a serious setback if only because Mr. Kracht already had too much on his plate. Moreover, constant bickering between the Executive Director and his senior colleagues (with the possible exception of Ms. Anne Rogers, who was soon to return to DIESA in New York) had become the order of the day, making life almost impossible for everyone.

That the Executive Director's last days in Rome were not his happiest is evident from the fact that he also appears to have antagonised the only remaining favourite at senior level, his one-time 'Special Representative', Mr. Uwe Kracht'. I had never suspected there had been any simmering dispute between them, until it finally erupted.

Matters came to a head when, on 16 June 1992, the Executive Director sent Mr. Kracht a sharp memo in which he accused him of insubordination. "Your recent intemperate memoranda to me", he said, "dealing with issues that we have already amply discussed, are insubordinate and suggest a repeat of your previous difficulties". What? *Previous* difficulties? All this was news to me.

Mr. Kracht replied angrily the following day, accusing the boss of exhibiting "the poorest thinkable judgement in management, rarely resorted to in any management situation". He ended by saying that he would refer the matter to the existing machinery for grievances and appeals procedures in New York.

His memo was dated 17 June 1992. Whatever transpired thereafter is anybody's guess. But it seems unlikely that an appeal was ever heard, or even launched, in New York, if only because within six months of these exchanges the Executive Director of the World Food Council, Mr. Gerald Ion Trant, had left the Council for good. We bade him "*a dieu!*" No love lost. No tears shed.

At his departure, he left me, whom he had earlier described as being in need of "close supervision" as Officer-in-Charge of the World Food Council, precisely the position he had found me in when he first reported for duty in Rome six years before. How ironical! The wheel of fortune had turned full circle. I did not know whether to laugh or cry.

CHAPTER XV

1991 – 1993
IN ROME AGAIN, AND BACK TO WORK

"I had prayed – and waited – long enough for this day to arrive...
The entire staff in Rome, with a few exceptions, applauded my
return and gave me a warm welcome"

Much as I had wanted – and fought – to return to Rome, I had long realized that when victory eventually did come (as it now had), the wounds it would leave behind would be slow to heal, and the scars would never entirely disappear. I was under no illusion whatever that my post in Rome as the Executive Director's immediate subordinate was going to be an easy one.

A remark made jokingly by a friend of mine kept ringing in my ears: "Don't deceive yourself, Peter. You and Gerry will never be comfortable bedfellows!"

I knew he was right; that although the battle had been won, the war was not yet over. I therefore came to Rome with all my ammunition intact, not in order to resume the fight, but in order to defend myself, just in case. I resolved *never to allow myself to stand in a position of weakness.*

I had made this resolve known the moment I received the letter inviting me to return to Rome. In his obvious reluctance to concede defeat, the Executive Director's 'invitation' was at best half-hearted; and at worst, ill-wishing. His attached memo to Mr. Ciss, who had succeeded Mr. Annan as Assistant Secretary-General, Human Resources Management, a memo copied to the U.N. top echelon, said, in effect, that I was unfit for the job, implying that his decision had been taken under duress.

One of the officials to whom the memo was copied was Ms Angela E.V. King, Director of Staff Administration and Training Division, Office of Human Resources Management, whose responsibility it was to send me the formal letter (or P.5 action, as it is called) re-assigning me to Rome.

My reply dated 1 November 1991 to her letter, copied to Mr.Ciss, Mr. Foran, and Mr. Trant, included the following passage:

"I notice that in spite of his own decision to reassign me to an important post in   Rome, Mr Trant states that he does not consider me a 'perfect match' for the post, and that he would not change the functions of a post 'simply to suit an individual'. These remarks bother me. Whether or not this was their intention, such remarks have three unfortunate effects on me. The first is the intimidation I feel, that I either perform or else! The second is my feeling that Mr. Trant is prejudging my performance even before I assume my new functions. It is as if Mr Trant is preparing the ground for the day when he can make a formal 'evaluation', decide that my performance is bad, and simply say to Mr. Ciss and Mr. Foran, 'I told you so'.

The third is the bad effect on morale his announcement is bound to have, on the part of my colleagues generally, but more especially on those who will be working under my supervision after being told by the Executive Director that I, their supervisor, fall short of the demands of my responsibilities.

I am most reluctant and a bit embarrassed to be writing this, but I am sure you can understand why I have had to do so for the record. For, apart from the fact that few people can claim to be a perfect match for the posts they hold, it is a rare departure from normal practice for a Chief Executive to extend this kind of 'welcome' to his immediate subordinate on the eve of assigning him important new responsibilities"   (See Annex 4.5)

Before returning to Rome, I did one more thing, although I knew pretty well that the Executive Director would not like it. I decided to lay bare the full contents of the JAB Report No. 820, so that every staff member in the WFC Secretariat in Rome would understand the truth of the matter.

In my covering letter dated 24 June 1991, circulated to all WFC staff in Rome, I stated, in part:

"As you are well aware, I have not participated in the normal activities of the WFC Secretariat for two years now. But this has been the Executive Director's choice, not mine. I have yet to be told why.

In 1989, the Executive Director took away my established post for the benefit of Mr. Vidal-Naquet, whom he styled Acting Deputy Executive Director. He reduced me to a supernumerary. I appealed to the Joint Appeals Board and his decision was set aside. Such are the facts, pure and simple. Do not, my dear friends, listen to rumours, half-truths or innuendoes from the grapevine.

Lastly, may I take this opportunity to salute you and to congratulate you all on your accomplishments at Bangkok last year and at Helsingor this year – two extremely demanding sessions in which I was not given the opportunity to share the burden with you. I have fond memories of our association together during our three beautiful years I was in Rome. One measure of the extent to which things have changed is that I could be out on a pleasure trip to Niagara Falls in Canada at a time all of you were busy with the ministerial session in Denmark"

I reported for duty in Rome on November 1, 1991, and got straight down to work. I had prayed and waited long enough for this day to arrive. There was literally a mountain of work ahead of me. The main agenda that preoccupied the whole WFC Secretariat during this time was preparations for the forthcoming Ministerial Conference scheduled to be held in Nairobi, Kenya, in June 1992. Incidentally, this Ministerial session turned out to be the last before the WFC was abolished, the last before the Executive Director was retired, and the last before the Secretariat staff scattered in all directions. In my new role as Chief, External Relations and Council Affairs, the major burden of organizing the conference rested squarely on my shoulders

Fortunately, the entire staff in Rome, with one or two exceptions, applauded my return and gave me a warm welcome. They were broadly sympathetic with me, and pleased that I had kept them informed and taken them into my confidence all along during my strained relations with the Executive Director. The JAB report I had circulated to them, plus my covering letter, had produced the desired effect – sympathy, and a spirit of mutual confidence.

Organizing ministerial sessions was for me a familiar activity. Working side by side with my colleagues, I supervised the documentation, made all the necessary contacts, and drafted for the Executive Director's signature all the letters of invitation addressed to Ministers and other top officials. Under the chairmanship of Mr. Issa Kalantari, Minister for Agriculture of the Islamic Republic of Iran, the Nairobi session in which, apart from the Executive Director, I was the central secretariat figure, passed without a hitch. Throughout the session – as indeed before, and after – relations between me and the Executive Director were business as usual – correct, but never warm.

At the concluding session in Nairobi, the Executive Director announced that he was retiring from the World Food Council and that I would be Officer-in-Charge of the Council until such time as the Secretary-General of the United Nations appointed a successor.

Of course no successor was ever appointed. The Council had outlived its usefulness. Gerald Ion Trant had, in effect, presided over the demise of the World Food Council. The secretariat was disbanded the following year, no subsequent ministerial session ever took place, and the World Food Council limped on, like a ghost, until 1996, when it was finally dissolved in the same way that in 1974 it had been created – by a resolution of the United Nations General Assembly. Its functions were taken over partly by the FAO and partly by the World Food Programme.

Chapter XVI
The Executive Director's last days in the Council

By any measure, the Executive Director's last days in the Council were not the happiest. Our strained relations apart, an unfortunate cleavage also developed between him and his other two senior colleagues, including the 'Acting Deputy Executive Director', his one time favourite French incumbent of my D-1 post, who had retired a year before my return to Rome. The other was the 'Special Representative of the Executive Director', a German national, who was still on board, and whose approved title was 'Chief, Policy Development and Economic Analysis'.

During the tenure of the previous Executive Director, Mr. Maurice Williams, these two high-level officials, together with myself, were all designated as Section Chiefs. At that time, both of them were junior to me by one notch, and the three of us worked happily together. The present Executive Director now decided to forge new titles (which were never approved by New York) in order to create the impression that a promotion had occurred, and so that in the resulting confusion the D-1 positions in the Council, especially mine, could be conveniently switched to a new incumbent. Such was the case with the glorified title of 'Acting Deputy Executive Director', created at a time when the staffing table did not even have an established post of Deputy Executive Director, to which anyone could be – or aspire to be – appointed in an acting capacity.

The title 'Special Representative of the Executive Director' was equally spurious and unacceptable, because in the United Nations it was a title normally reserved for prominent diplomats appointed by the Secretary-General as his Special Representatives. As an appointee of the Secretary-General, the Executive Director himself was not entitled to have a 'Special Representative'.

The third senior position was that of Secretary to the Council. This was an existing post encumbered by an American lady, Ms. Anne Rogers, at P-5 level, who was being groomed to take over the D-1 post left vacant by the retirement of the 'Acting Deputy Executive Director'.

Unhappily for the Executive Director, his carefully crafted plan which would have seen me dejected from the Council, or else encumbering a P-5 post while being paid a salary at D-1 level (an idea flatly rejected by Mr. Foran), with Anne Rogers taking the D-1 post, was wholly fouled up by the Secretary-General's insistence that I be transferred to Rome *without any further delay* to encumber the vacant D-1 post. It was my appearance in Rome at the beginning of November 1991 that threw a spanner into the works!

(i) First sign of sabotage nipped in the bud.

One of my earliest complaints against the Executive Director shortly after I reported for duty in Rome concerned Ms. Anne Rogers, my immediate subordinate in the External Relations and Council Affairs (ERCA) unit. It happened that the Executive Director had given me an important office assignment with the usual pressure of deadlines. I had scheduled an urgent meeting of the professional staff of my unit, of whom Ms. Anne Rogers was the senior-most, to take place in the next few days. Precisely at the time I needed her most, the Executive Director withdrew her services from me by granting her written authorization, without my approval or knowledge, to go on mission in New York for a week to monitor the proceedings of the General Assembly, followed by two weeks home leave in Detroit.

I could not – and would not, of course – try to stop her, but I interpreted the Executive Director's action as deliberate sabotage of my work. I reasoned to myself that if this was the first sign of what I was to expect, then my only response should be to nip it in the bud. Therefore, no sooner had she departed than I dropped a bombshell. On 16 December 1991, I lashed out at the Executive Director, as follows:

"Considering the verbal assurances you gave me after you had read my memo to Ms. Angela King dated 1 November 1991, and my own verbal assurance that I would forget the past and work loyally and faithfully under your leadership, I did not expect that I would be writing so soon to protest to you against your attitude and treatment of me in my new position as the Council's Chief of External Relations and Council Affairs, to which you appointed me less than two months ago.

Because of the depressingly large number of time-consuming memos one sees in the World Food Council, I shall try to make mine as short as possible.

As I write, Ms. Anne Rogers, my immediate subordinate in this unit of three professionals, is in New York, reportedly to attend the last week of the General Assembly and, in the absence of Ms. Kate Newell, listen in on anything that delegations may be saying regarding the future of the World Food Council. After a week there, she proceeds on two weeks' home leave to Detroit, returning to Rome on 6 or 7 January, depending on the availability of flights.

These arrangements were authorized by you as Executive Director, and it would therefore not be proper for me to comment, ex post facto, on their propriety or otherwise.

However, I take strong exception to the fact that Ms. Rogers did not discuss and clear her plans with me in advance. I also take exception to the fact that you yourself, knowing that her travel plans did not have my approval (or even knowledge) as section Chief, went ahead and authorized them just the same. Lastly, I regret to see that you did so at a time when you knew that you had instructed me to produce a programme of work for the Unit, and precisely when I had scheduled a meeting for Monday, 16 December, with Ms. Rogers to discuss the draft before its submission to you the following Thursday. To my surprise, the first time I became aware of Ms. Rogers' plans was when she walked into my office late Friday morning (13 December), showed me photocopies of authorization papers signed by you, and then walked away to collect her tickets from the travel agent.

I would like to dispel any possible misunderstanding, just in case. My main worry is not that I sorely miss Ms. Rogers' contribution. With or without her, the work you assigned me will continue. The crux of my complaint is, firstly, that she should have failed to clear her mission-cum-home leave plans with me in the first instance as her immediate supervisor, and, secondly, that you should have seen fit to authorize it in spite of that. I find this not only procedurally irregular, but very embarrassing because it totally undermines my role and status as Chief of the Unit, and humiliates me in the eyes of my subordinates. I am most anxious to have your assurance that this does not set a precedent.

It is unacceptable that you as Executive Director should assign me "most important responsibilities in Rome" (your own phrase), and then proceed to take away from me the authority I need to discharge those responsibilities".

Mr. Trant would not let such sharp criticism go unanswered. Exactly one week later, on 20 January 1992, came his reply:

"I should like to refer to your memorandum to me dated 16 December 1991.

Ms. Rogers' home leave plans were authorized by me, as her immediate supervisor at the time, five months before your appointment as Chief, External Relations and Council Affairs. Furthermore, the authority to require that home leave be taken in conjunction with travel on official business rests with the head of office. However, as I recall, you were consulted before final arrangements were made for Ms. Rogers to attend the last week of the General Assembly (in the absence of Ms. Newell, Officer-in-Charge of WFC's Liaison Office in New York) and you did not raise any objections.

In any event, you are correct when you state that it is not proper for you to comment ex post facto on the propriety of decisions which I have made in accordance with the relevant delegations of authority.

Nobody at the WFC secretariat wishes to embarrass or humiliate you in the eyes of your subordinates. You may want to give some thought for the feelings and reputations of others. If anyone has the right to feel aggrieved by your gratuitous criticism it is Ms. Anne Rogers, an honest, competent, committed and hard working staff member. I therefore disagree with your assessment, based on barely one month on the job, that you will not sorely miss her contribution to the work of your unit.

I regret that you have made such a minor issue into a point of contention within the WFC secretariat and even outside, by copying your complaints to the Director-General for Development and International Economic Co-operation. I doubt very much that the United Nations' second most senior official has any interest in the matter you raised".

I must confess that, given our past relationship, it was impossible for me to give Mr. Trant any benefit of the doubt. There was no longer any mutual trust, but only mutual suspicion, between us. I felt certain that after my return to Rome, he was bound to use his 'big muscle' as a boss to settle scores with me. His sole ambition was to try to demonstrate to the world that I was unable to fulfil my assignment in Rome, and that the decision to send me there – which had been forced down his throat – was a mistake. I therefore expected he would do anything openly or clandestinely to sabotage my work.

It was in that light that I viewed his withdrawal of Ms. Anne Rogers' services with suspicion, and why I laid the blame squarely, not on her, but on Mr. Trant personally. In the same vein, I regarded his response to my letter as sheer cover-up, a tissue of lies and excuses (for example, his blatant lie that I had been consulted about her mission to New York, and had not raised any objection).

But the worst part was not the deterioration in relations between Mr.Trant and myself – which was not news any more. The real tragedy lay in the fact that this unhealthy state of affairs was spreading, like a virus, to the entire top echelon of the WFC secretariat. Starting with the Executive Director himself, the entire leadership of this small but once vibrant secretariat appeared to be in shambles.

(ii) Mutual recriminations among the senior staff of the WFC secretariat

Precisely at the critical time when the future of the World Food Council was at stake, and under scrutiny by an ad hoc committee of the United Nations General Assembly in New York, the section chiefs of the WFC secretariat in Rome were not seeing eye to eye: they would not get together to discuss, let alone agree on, proposals for the Council's future work programme. Inter-sectional feuding was rife; and an atmosphere of mistrust prevailed between the External Relations and Council Affairs (ERCA) section led by Anne Rogers, and the Policy Development and Economic Analysis (PDEA) section, led by Mr. Uwe Kracht. And there was no leader to call the disputants to order.

These differences were exposed in recriminations against Mr Kracht contained in a letter dated 14 August 1992, addressed to me by Ms. Anne Rogers, at a time when she was Officer-in-Charge of ERCA, Mr. Kracht was Chief of PDEA, and I was Officer-in-Charge of WFC. Her letter is a succinct description of what she called the "lack of collegiality and the abundance of professional mistrust" in the WFC secretariat.

This is what she said to me:

"I should like to report to you on the work of the External Relations and Council Affairs Unit during your absence from Rome on mission and leave, 8 July- 18 August 1992. I refer specifically to ERCA's, and my own, contribution to the preparations for the ad hoc committee on the future of the WFC, scheduled for September in New York.

1. In my capacity as Officer-in-Charge of ERCA I have attended the three regional group meetings with Rome representatives

of WFC Member States organized by Mr. Kracht to discuss secretariat preparations for the <u>ad hoc</u> committee. At Mr Kracht's request, I have written summary notes on these meetings ,which were held on 3, 6 and 10 August (the meeting with Latin American and Caribbean States planned for 31 July was cancelled); copies of these notes have been sent to you.

2. Also as requested by Mr. Kracht, I have been in contact with the United States Embassy in Rome concerning procedures for obtaining visas for President Kalantari and his advisors to travel to New York in September. Please see the file of correspondence on this which I have prepared for you.

3, As for the preparation of the secretariat document to be presented to the <u>ad hoc</u> committee, my participation has been limited to providing comments to Mr. Kracht on his 20 and 21 July draft outlines. Until two days ago, I had not received any further outline nor have I to date seen any draft at all, for comment or even information. I have not been sent the "summary tables" of reform proposals which I know exist and which I know have already been faxed to UN Headquarters. I have not even been given copies of all the country statements on which these tables are based. And, contrary to your fax to me of 16 July, Mr. Kracht has not shared with me the information he has received on ECOSOC and other relevant discussions in New York, despite my written request to him on 24 July and numerous oral reminders.

4. After three weeks of repeated requests to see a new outline or draft sections of the report, I was sent on12 August a revised draft outline which differs significantly from the last outline I saw on 21 July. This new outline was not sent to me nor to

ERCA for comments; in fact, it was attached to a letter from Mr Kracht to Mr. Patrizio Civili, Director of the Office of the Secretary-General and Secretary of the ACC, which had already been faxed to New York. Also contained in the letter was the information that Ms. Jane Jopling, Director in the Office of the Secretary-General, would be coming to Rome, apparently very shortly, for consultation with WFC. This had not been communicated to me nor to ERCA.

5. Today, when Mr. Kracht told some staff in my presence that the report would be "finalized" tonight, I again asked to see a draft. His reply – also in the presence of WFC staff members – was that this and the background material it was based on was "confidential". I said to him and I should like to say to you, that I, as a senior officer in the WFC secretariat and someone whom you have put in charge of the External Relations and Council Affairs Unit for the past six weeks, find this response insulting to ERCA, to my personal and professional integrity, and to your own managerial judgement.

6. I find these events unfortunate and unnecessary, the more so since they reflect the lack of collegiality and the abundance of professional mistrust that is so evident in the WFC secretariat. I should also like to point out the obvious unimportance Mr. Kracht assigns to the role of the ERCA unit in this very crucial time in the Council's existence.

7. Finally, I should also like to mention something which Mr. Kracht may raise with you. He said to me today that I had "refused to contribute a chapter" to the secretariat report on the reforms ongoing in the United Nations system. On this question, I draw your attention to my memorandum to Mr.

Kracht of 24 July 1992, the date by which he wanted this input. As you very well know, on 24 July ECOSOC was still in session in New York and negotiations were scheduled to continue for another full week. I therefore replied to Mr. Kracht, by his due date, my opinion that "…the uncertainty and inconclusive nature of the ongoing ECOSOC debate on institutional and intergovernmental restructuring and reform makes it virtually impossible <u>at this stage</u> to provide anything like a clear and comprehensive statement of agreed – or even disagreed – positions" (Underlining added). I did not refuse to write a note on UN reforms; I only said that I thought it was rather pointless to try to do so by 24 July. I thought my views on the preparation of the paper were being requested and that such important considerations as the dates of ECOSOC were relevant.

8. I have never received a reply nor any response to this memorandum. I had also asked – again in writing – in this memorandum to receive copies of the briefing notes on ECOSOC that you and Ms. Newell were sending from New York. To date I have not. In fact, I have just this week discovered that a 42-page summary of the high-level segment of ECOSOC which was faxed to Mr. Kracht on 7 July has been circulating among PDEA staff for the past month and a half and purposively not been sent to me. I have pointed out to Mr. Kracht - to no effect – the irrationality of his request to summarise proposals, documents and decisions that he refuses to make available to me.

I believe you, as Officer-in-Charge of the WFC secretariat and Chief of ERCA, should be aware of these developments during your absence from Rome. I trust that you will agree with me that the fact that the ERCA, and its senior officer, have been denied any significant role during this most important period of the Council's work is not only regrettable but also unhelpful to our common aims".

Ms. Rogers' letter was merely a formal articulation of what was already clear beyond doubt, namely, that the WFC secretariat was in a state of disarray. Naturally, as Officer-in-Charge of the Council, I knew that it was incumbent on me to do whatever I could to put things right. But I had hardly had time to even think about it before everything was overtaken by events.

(iii) I am relieved of my duties as Officer-in-Charge

It happened that at around this time preparations were under way for the Council's participation in a high-level International Conference on Nutrition organized by the FAO. Nutrition had always been a subject of high priority to the Council, especially the policy question regarding access to food aid to conflict areas. The conference offered one more opportunity for the Council, as a high-level policy organ, to make a strong pronouncement on the issue, and I made sure that this was done. A statement prepared carefully by my colleagues and I, and delivered by me as head of the WFC delegation, was well received and even hit the headlines.

But as soon as the conference ended, we learned that U.N. Headquarters had taken exception to the statement. Without any oral or written communication with me, the next thing I saw was a cable from Headquarters accusing me of indiscipline and poor judgement, for having used my position to advance my own personal views. I was not asked or expected to respond to the accusation: I was simply informed that the Secretary-General had decided that I should henceforth cease to be Officer-in-Charge of the Council.

That was it. Neither then, nor subsequently, did anyone pinpoint to me exactly which part of my statement was unacceptable, and it remains a mystery who at U.N. Headquarters actually objected to my statement, and why.

As if the ghost of the (now former) Executive Director was still haunting me, it was apparent that misfortunes were continuing to dog me even after his departure from Rome. I wondered at the time – indeed I wonder to this day – whether he might not have secretly contacted the authorities in New York and tried – successfully this time - to wreak vengeance on me, even as he bemoaned his own fate. The truth may never become known, but nothing can be ruled out.

My instinctive reaction was to shrug it off, step aside resignedly, and let the future take care of itself. But my colleagues in Rome decided otherwise. They were determined to rebut the accusation. For once, and perhaps for the last time, they were able to rally together in my support, and send the following trite message to the Secretary-General:

"To : The Secretary-General   Date: December 16, 1992

Subject: Mr. Temu's removal as Officer-in-Charge of the World Food Council

We have learned, with regret, that our colleague Peter Temu has been relieved of his duties as Officer-in –Charge on the grounds that he used his position to air personal views in the statement he read at the International Conference on Nutrition.

This is an absolutely false allegation. Mr. Temu did not use his position as Officer-in-Charge to advance his own personal views. He did his duty as head of the WFC delegation by delivering a statement prepared for him by the secretariat staff on behalf of the Council. We are shocked that this action can be described as an 'inexcusable lack of judgement and discipline'.

The three of us, under Mr. Kracht's supervision, worked on the ICN statement very thoroughly. It went through several drafts before we finally agreed on its contents. This is the procedure we have always followed. As Officer-in-Charge, Mr. Temu could have made further changes of the text if he had wanted. In fact, he did not. He added nothing and took away nothing. What is more, nothing in the statement reflects the personal views of anyone of us.

In the circumstances, we consider it grossly unjust that Mr. Temu should have been punished and humiliated for an offence he has not committed, and, knowing the high importance you attach to staff morale, we sincerely hope that the situation can be rectified"

Of course the situation was never rectified. Within a few days I stepped down as Officer-in-Charge in favour of Mr Abdou Diouf who arrived from Headquarters to take up a post with the International Fund for Agricultural Development (IFAD), but was temporarily also assigned nominal responsibility as Officer-in-Charge of the World Food Council.

CHAPTER XVII

1993 TO 1996
AT THE ECA MULPOC IN LUSAKA:
SMOOTH SAILING TO THE END

"We lived as friends, and went about our task happily and harmoniously, inspired by a genuine spirit of team work"

By the beginning of 1993, the entire Temu/Trant drama was over, and only the memory of it was left. The Executive Director had retired from the Council, and presumably returned to his home in Canada. There was no love lost between us. We severed our ties permanently.

The secretariat of the World Food Council – if not the Council itself – was falling apart, with each individual staff member trying his/her best to seek alternative employment wherever he/she could find it. In the ongoing UN restructuring exercise, it was already known that the functions hitherto performed by the WFC secretariat would come within the jurisdiction of the new Department of Policy Co-ordination and Sustainable Development, based at UN Headquarters in New York. A few of the secretariat staff did manage to find a niche there, including, if I remember, Ms. Anne Rogers. Most of the senior staff in Rome, however, ended up elsewhere, and not necessarily within the United Nations system.

As for me, I had no desire to return to New York, even if I had been offered a place there. After all the trauma I had been through, to say nothing of this latest humiliation, and given that I had only three years left to retirement age, my primary interest was to return to Africa, to live and work a little nearer home. Working and living in Europe and America for ten years running was long enough, and I felt it was time for a change.

My first instinct was to see if I could return to my former employer, the ECA, and I contacted them accordingly. To my delight, the ECA responded promptly, saying that they were prepared to reabsorb me on their staff, and to post me to Lusaka, the Zambian capital, to be the new Director of the Multinational Programming and Operational Centre (MULPOC) for Eastern and Southern Africa. My acceptance was immediate. Once more, fortune had smiled on me. The wheel of fortune had turned full circle. I had started off my UN career with the ECA in 1977, and I would end it with the ECA in 1996! My WFC assignments in Rome, New York and Rome again, and their ups and downs, now seemed to me to have been a mere (if rather bumpy) detour.

One major advantage of my returning to ECA was the fact that in the official personnel records at UN Headquarters – and these records are extremely well kept – I continued to be regarded as a staff member whose service to the UN had continued unbroken, since my recruitment in 1977 until my retirement in 1996. The fact that in the meantime I had, for one reason or another, switched jobs from ECA to WFC, and from WFC back to ECA, working at successive duty stations, did not seem to matter. If anything, these movements, by adding to my international experience, may even have enhanced my professional image, if not my retirement benefits.

The assignment at Lusaka was a pleasant one: it was smooth sailing, all through. The Government of Zambia accorded me the status of head of a diplomatic mission, identical with that accorded to foreign diplomats of ambassadorial rank, with all the privileges and immunities that go with it. Such diplomatic recognition would have been impossible in Rome, and unthinkable in New York.

The MULPOC office which I headed for three years was the largest of five MULPOCs which ECA had established to cover the various sub-regions of Africa. The membership of the Lusaka-based MULPOC consisted of 23 Eastern and Southern African states. As Director of the MULPOC, my task was, in addition to running the office, to organize, on behalf of the Executive Secretary of ECA, conferences of Ministers, which were usually preceded by meetings of inter-governmental committees of experts. These meetings were convened to discuss, approve, and follow up on sub-regional economic co-operation projects, which were normally initiated by the MULPOC staff, but sometimes also by the staff at ECA headquarters or by officials of ministries responsible for economic cooperation within the member states.

From time to time, depending on demand and the availability of funds, I would, with the Executive Secretary's approval, either go personally or send one of my colleagues on mission to selected countries, in order to monitor the implementation of agreed projects, and prepare documentation for subsequent meetings.

There was no conflict or animosity of any kind among our small team of (wholly African) professional staff. We lived as friends, and went about our task happily and harmoniously, inspired by a genuine spirit of team work.

Occasionally, the ghost of my rough and turbulent years in Rome and New York would rear its ugly head, if only in my imagination. But my life and work in the Zambian capital was a source of great satisfaction for me, and a fitting ending to my United Nations career, which lasted until my retirement in February 1996.

Postscript.

I wanted to write a "Concluding Chapter" to this book, but in the end decided not to. While the book has definite object lessons, for employers and their employees, for bosses and their subordinates, which call for concluding remarks, I thought it best to let the reader himself ponder them in his mind and draw his own conclusions.

Some have suggested that the book would have conveyed its message more forcefully if it had been written in the form of a play, with the Executive Director and the author as the heroes of the drama. Well, maybe. The door remains open.

THE END

ANNEXES

INDEX TO THE ANNEXES

3.5 Letter dated 18 October 1991 from Mr. Trant to me

Annex 4. The Executive Director's qualified 'welcome' to me to return to Rome.

4.1 Letter dated 20 September 1991 from Mr. Trant to me
4.2 Letter dated 11 October 1991 from me to Mr. Trant
4.3 Letter dated 20 September 1991 from Mr. Trant to Mr. Ciss
4.4 Letter dated 26 September 1991 from Ms. King to me
4.5 Letter dated 1 November 1991 from me to Ms. King

Annex 5. Official record of the author's Performance Evaluation Reports: 1977-1986

Annex 6. The seniority ladder and official designations of United Nations professional .staff.

ANNEX I:

SELECTED CORRESPONDENCE
RELATING TO MY JOB CRISIS.

The following is the <u>core</u> correspondence relating to the struggle to save my job. The correspondence begins with the Executive Director's letter to me dated 12 June 1989 which sparked off the struggle by saying that I should leave the Council by the end of the year. It ends with his letter of 'surrender' dated 20 September 1991 which welcomes me back to Rome. In between these two dates, is a whole barrage of letters involving different parties, which shows how the crisis evolved and how it was finally resolved.

1.1 Letter dated 12 June 1989 from Mr. Trant to me.

"Dear Peter,

I feel I have to share with you the following.

Since I took over my post as Executive Director and sent you to our New York office – as you, yourself, had suggested – I find that we have not achieved what I had originally expected. I was hoping that our secretariat would be a more active presence at United Nations headquarters, both with government representatives and the UN secretariat departments involved in economic and social issues.

Your reporting has not kept me fully abreast on what was happening in New York at a moment when the whole system is being reviewed, not only because of the financial crisis but also at the substantive level, and leads to a re-organization of the whole UN system which may affect the Council's future.

The co-ordination issue, of special importance to us, has not been really followed through, in particular through an adequate reporting of the preparation and the results of the ACC meetings which, even if we are not a full member, have an important impact on our work. The preparation of the International Development Strategy and the substantive inter-agency consultation held in New York related to the follow-up on UNPAAERD did not get the full attention they should have had from your side.

I do not recall any special reporting or initiative taken by you during the last two years which have helped in shaping up the WFC contribution to the UN documents or our own. For instance, there are a number of forthcoming events, such as the UN General Assembly Special Session on International Economic Co-operation 1990, the forthcoming meeting of the Special Programme of Action of the Least Developed Countries, and others on which I would have hoped that you would have, by yourself, started to give me advice and suggestions.

Also, for instance, I have noted that your reporting on the last ECA Conference of Ministers in Addis Ababa does not relate to our ongoing or future work on what we are doing with African countries, and you did not provide specific ideas or suggestions to see how we could use part of the ECA conclusions in our future programme of work.

At the same time, the preparation of the report of the last WFC session left a lot to be desired, as it appears that the staff involved received contradictory instructions.

I really feel that – while I recognize that you have a number of qualities which could be useful in a more adequate context – you might consider looking around in New York (or elsewhere) for another post by the end of the year. I would not like to make any decision which could damage you either professionally or personally, but I believe it would be of mutual benefit if you would consider seriously such a possibility.

Yours sincerely,
Gerald I. Trant
Executive Director"

1.2: Letter dated 18 July 1989 from me to Mr. Trant in reply to his of 12 June 1989

"Mr. Gerald I. Trant
Executive Director
World Food Council, Rome
Dear Gerry,

Thank you for your letter of 12 June 1989.

This is an interim reply. I take it that your letter does not call for specific answers to specific questions, but provides an opportunity for useful reflection.

This note is therefore neither recriminatory nor defensive. It is positive and, I hope, constructive. My motto is to get on with the job and strive for improvement, while keeping in mind the contents of your letter. I have, in this spirit, decided to institute a monthly reporting system, beginning with the June 1989 Report which I have already sent to you under cover of my letter dated 13 July 1989. This will be followed by regular monthly updates on activities in New York which are of significant relevance to the Council. I hope that this procedure – among other innovations which I am going to introduce – is a move in the right direction. I might also suggest for your consideration your designating someone at your end who would bring to my attention anything my reports may have overlooked, or on which further information or views are needed, in the light of knowledge in Rome, so that I can take prompt action to fill the gap. This kind of feedback will ensure that my reports to you will have continuing utility and relevance.

Since the sole source of your dissatisfaction with me stems from the period I have served in New York, I feel impelled to make the following observation. In just two years we have, in my view, come a long way from the day when in 1987 I sat in my first CPC meeting here at U.N. Headquarters, under the searching scrutiny of the ECOSOC Special Commission. In that meeting, I had to answer a barrage of questions against the Council spearheaded by two influential delegations which believed that the Council should either be abolished or be absorbed by the FAO, and said so without mincing words. You will recall that I kept you in very close touch with developments then. There was of course a lot of confusion and misunderstanding concerning the role of the Council which we did our utmost to dispel. Confidence building is a difficult art. It took time, patience and perseverance, but in the end we did it.

Judging by the results, and considering the problem we faced, it appears to me that this office has done quite well, though I am far from complacent, and I would be the last to suggest that the credit is ours alone. It is not by chance that there is now much greater appreciation in New York circles of the role of the Council and much more respect for its image. Criticism at recent sessions of the CPC and ACABQ has been muted, if not entirely absent. While most of the credit goes to you as Executive Director, I find it hard to accept that the contribution made by the New York Office is small or negligible. I believe in fact that it has been significant – thanks to its active presence at United Nations Headquarters and its rapport with government representatives as well as with secretariat officials. I am aware that your own perception is just the opposite and I respect your views. But I cannot agree with them.

The idea of my leaving the Council at the end of the year is something that I cannot seriously entertain. My commitment to the Council and to the United Nations is total. My devotion to my career is complete. I have a very good professional track record, and all my supervisors, down the years, can vouch for this. At a time when I have less than two years to my formal retirement (I recall confiding in you my intention to retire at 55), I could not even think of changing jobs.

I am grateful for your assurance that you will not do anything to damage me personally or professionally. The truth is that nothing would be more damaging to me than to abandon, two years before my formal retirement, a professional and pensionable career which I have performed well, for so long, and on which the future of my entire family depends. I know that I am in New York at your pleasure. I can only repeat my assurance that whether in this or any other capacity, I will continue to serve the Council loyally, take criticism in a constructive spirit, and always strive to do better. This is a positive

approach which is good for the Council and, I believe, for all concerned..
But dropping my job is an entirely different proposition, and I crave
your understanding not to pursue it.

Yours sincerely,

Peter E. Temu

Chief

World Food Council Office in New York"

1.3: Letter dated 21 July 1989 from me to Mr. Kofi Annan.

"To: Mr. Kofi Annan,

Assistant Secretary-General

Office of Human Resources Management

From: Peter E. Temu

Chief, World Food Council Liaison Office in New York

Thank you for letting me see you. It is an opportunity which my
supervisor, Mr. Trant, has not himself given me in spite of his alleged
dissatisfaction with my work.

I attach his letter to me dated 12 June 1989 and my interim reply
to it, which both denies his charges and rejects his idea of my leaving
the Council.

I also attach a brief reference to my official performance evaluations
for all the years I have worked with the United Nations. This includes
Mr. Trant's first, and so far only, official performance evaluation of
me filed with your office.

On the basis of that record, I was not only given permanent status in 1984 – a status not easily earned by professionals at that age and level – but I was promoted to D-1 in 1985.. Naturally, I am proud of this record, as any employee would be. I may add that I had an equally good record in my own country, where I had risen to the top of my planning ministry in 1974, and later headed a successful parastatal institute, the Institute of Finance Management, before President Nyerere formally released me to join ECA in 1977. What was intended as a temporary secondment turned out to be a life-long international career.

I say I am proud of my record, because this is how others, my seniors – including, at first Mr. Trant himself – have always seen my work. For me to be ashamed of that record would be to be ashamed of each and every one of those supervisors, and indeed to be ashamed of the United Nations. This I cannot and will not do.

My faith in and commitment to the World Food Council and the United Nations is complete and unshaken. All my previous supervisors – and they can all still be reached - can vouch for my character, ability and integrity. In view of Mr. Trant's own praise of my work when I was in charge of the WFC before his assumption of office, and the record just stated, I am totally perplexed to see him make complete U-turn to the point of wishing me to quit my job. Whatever his real reason, I find it hard to believe that it has anything to do with my performance in New York. Might it be that I am being pushed out to make room for someone else? Only time will tell.

Since I came here, he and I have met many times, in Rome, New York, Nicosia and Cairo. Not once has he said a word against my performance. If he had, I would in the course of normal conversation have replied to any queries. Instead, his complaints have invariably appeared afterwards in personal letters to me, which are often couched in general terms and make the most sweeping allegations. If his letter of 12 June 1989 had made specific charges, duly substantiated, I could, and am still now ready, to refute them. Or if he had made a formal performance evaluation report – and one has been due since April 1989 – and graded my performance to reflect his present biased attitude of mind, I would have rebutted it. But he has chosen to do neither of these things. In this way he is able to use his position as supervisor and his access to you to have it both ways, that is, achieve his objective without the "inconvenience" of talking to me directly.

Finally, let me say that I have always understood and recognized Mr. Trant's right and privilege as my manager to deploy me anywhere and in any way he wants within the Council. My sole interest is to serve the United Nations and do it better, each day, if possible. Despite his strictures, I am not demoralized: I am willing to accept and able to discharge even higher responsibilities in the United Nations. I regret, however, that Mr. Trant, while refusing to make any formal evaluation of my performance since coming to New York, prefers to undermine my credibility by writing damaging quasi-personal and quasi-official memos, so that when he does eventually write the long awaited official evaluation, it can become his last, the damage having been done.

I do not believe the United Nations will agree to dispose of me so easily, and, win or lose, I intend to use the established machinery to the last. I am confident however that with your advice and assistance this will not be necessary."

1.4: Letter dated 28 July 1989 from Mr. Trant to me

"Dear Mr. Temu,

May I take this opportunity to notify you that you have been determined to be against a transitional post (UNT-01018-E-D-2-001).

I sincerely hope that it will be possible for you to be laterally re-assigned.

Yours sincerely,

Gerald I. Trant

Executive Director.

cc: Mr. K. Annan, Assistant Secretary-General, OHRM".

1.5: Letter dated 8 September 1989 from Mr. Annan to me.

"Dear Mr. Temu,

The Office of Human Resources Management has been informed by WFC, in accordance with Administrative Instruction ST/AI/353 of 18 July 1988 on the internal reassignment of staff, that you are on a transitional post slated to be abolished by 31 December 1989.

We have placed your name on a list of staff to receive priority placement under the vacancy management and staff redeployment system. A copy of this list has been given to the members of the Appointments and Promotion Body concerned. Your recruitment and Placement Officer, Mr. Luiz Carlos Da Costa, is directly responsible for adding your name to the list of candidates for suitable posts. You are also urged to make your own efforts to identify suitable advertised vacancies which match your qualifications, professional experience and level and to apply for them.

Under the vacancy management system, it is possible that if selected for a post you may be expected to move from your current office or department to another or even to another duty station. You will be expected to co-operate fully with the Office of Human Resources Management in trying to find another post and/or in moving to a new department, office or duty station.

You may be interested to know that since departments and offices started to identify staff on "non-core" posts, over 20 professional staff, or about one-third, on transitional posts have been placed on "core" posts, i.e., posts which will continue to be authorized after 31 December 1989.

Please be assured that OHRM will keep you fully informed of progress made in seeking a suitable core post for you.

Yours sincerely,.

Kofi A. Annan

Assistant SecretaryGeneral

for Human Resources Management".

1.6: Letter dated 22 September 1989 from me to Mr. Annan

"Dear Mr. Annan,

I acknowledge receipt of your letter to me dated 6 September 1989.

I regret to say that the decision of the Executive Director of the World Food Council is unjust, discriminatory and taken in bad faith. My post has not been abolished, but simply given to someone else.

The World Food Council Liaison Office in New York, of which I am the head, has not been abolished. All that has happened is that, for reasons that have yet to be revealed, the Executive Director has singled me out for elimination, not only from the World Food Council Liaison Office in New York, but from the Council itself. His decision is therefore unacceptable to me. Please treat this letter as my notice to you of my intention to contest his decision.

I feel sad to reflect that, despite my appeals, you have seen fit to bless his decision by writing to me the letter you have.

Yours sincerely,
Peter E. Temu"

1.7: Letter dated 7 December 1989 from Mr. Annan to me.

"Dear Mr. Temu,

Now that the post reduction exercise mandated by the General Assembly is approaching its final stage, I believe it appropriate to outline the procedures envisaged for the immediate future and to dispel any misconceptions and allay any undue concerns that may have arisen.

As we all know, the Secretary-General has always maintained, and continues to maintain, that to the maximum extent possible the staff reduction mandated by the General Assembly should be achieved by attrition. Over the course of 1988 and 1989, intensive efforts have been made to find alternative assignments for staff on posts to be abolished. In more than a hundred cases, staff members have already been re-assigned to posts that will continue to be budgeted beyond 31 December 1989.

There remain, however, a number of staff members including you, for whom an alternative assignment or other solution is still pending, in as much as you are currently encumbering a non-core post, that is, a post scheduled to be abolished by the end of 1989. Although we are aware of the anxiety that this information may have caused, as an Administration we would have been less than candid if we had not made the situation clear, and thus engaged the co-operation of the staff members involved in seeking a solution to each case.

In this connection, I would like to emphasize two very important points. First, staff members on non-core posts were generally identified by departmental retrenchment panels on the basis of the criteria set out in administrative instruction ST/AI/353. Second, the notification referred to above in no way implies that all such staff members will have their appointments terminated at the end of the year.

To expand on the last point, the following are some of the measures the Secretary-General proposes to take to safeguard the interests of the staff concerned.

Staff members on permanent appointments who will reach retirement age in 1990 may serve until their normal date of retirement. For other staff on probationary or permanent appointments, or with more than five years on fixed-term appointments, every effort will continue to be made to find other assignments for which they are qualified. Since a number of core posts are currently vacant and normal turn-over will create additional opportunities for placement in the coming months, there are good prospects of success in cases where qualifications and experience match the requirements of the function. Furthermore, to facilitate the process outside recruitment will be allowed only on a very selective basis until all these staff members for whom suitable assignments can be found have been placed.

Staff members for whom other assignments cannot be found may be eligible for the separation benefits recommended by the Staff Management Committee at its 1988 session and approved by the Secretary-General. In general, these involve payment of the indemnity provided for in the Staff Rules plus 50 per cent, and an additional compensation in lieu of notice. Staff members who wish to be considered for such separation arrangements should discuss their eligibility with their Executive Officers and indicate this preference to them in writing by 31 January 1990 at the latest.

As regards staff members who were appointed prior to the institution of the recruitment freeze (1 January 1987) and have served more than three years but less than five on fixed-term appointments, unless their Departments make other arrangements to continue their service, they will be eligible at the expiry of their appointments for the indemnity envisaged for temporary appointments in annex III to the Staff Regulations, increased by 50 per cent.

For obvious considerations of fairness, it has been decided that staff members who separate with the special termination benefits mentioned above may not be considered for reappointment for a period of three years beginning on the date of separation.

I would suggest that you immediately consult your Executive and Administrative Officer, or your Personnel or Recruitment and Placement Officer, to obtain further clarification and guidance on the options available to you, and on what you can do to assist in solving the situation in your best interest.

I sincerely hope that this letter has helped in some measure to reassure you and clarify your situation. The staff of the Office of Human Resources Management and your department or office stand ready to assist you during this difficult period.

Yours sincerely,

Kofi A. Annan

Assistant Secretary-General

for Human Resources Management".

1.8: Letter dated 22 January 1990 from me to Mr. Annan in reply to his of 7 December1989.

"To: Mr. Kofi Annan

Assistant Secretary-General

Office of Human Resources Management

From: Peter E. Temu

World Food Council

Thank you for your confidential letter dated 7 December 1989 clarifying the options I face as an incumbent of a non-core post. Your letter came when I was on home leave from which I have just returned. It is only now that I am able to follow it up.

As suggested by you, I am consulting my Executive Officer or my Personnel Officer for further clarification and guidance and will revert to you soonest. Unless they can respond quickly and adequately to my queries, I shall have to seek from you an extension of the January 31 deadline. I am sure you will agree that this matter, on which my entire future hangs, is too important to be rushed or lightly dismissed.

Your letter has emphasized to me a very important point, namely, that "staff members on non-core posts were generally identified by departmental retrenchment panels on the basis of the criteria set out in administrative instruction ST/AI/353". I wish to place on record that in my particular case the whole exercise was carried out unilaterally and arbitrarily by the Executive Director, in complete disregard of that administrative instruction. You are aware that I have already protested formally against this action".

1.9: Letter dated 21 February 1990 from me to Mr. Annan

"Dear Mr. Annan,

On 22 September 1989 I wrote to you to complain about my Executive Director's decision to change my post. I stated:

"I regret to say that the decision of the Executive Director of the World Food Council is unjust, discriminatory and taken in bad faith. My post has not been abolished, but simply given to someone else. My World Food Council Liaison Office in New York, of which I am the head, has not been abolished. All that has happened is that, for reasons that have yet to be revealed, the Executive Director has singled me out for elimination, not only from the World Food Council Liaison Office in New York, but from the Council itself. His decision is therefore unacceptable to me. Please treat this letter as my notice to you of my intention to contest this decision".

Since that time I have not heard from you or him as to the reason why my post is to be taken away and handed over to another staff member.

Because of the seemingly fruitful discussions between you, the Executive Director and myself towards the end of last year, I was led to believe that no administrative action would be taken until a mutually agreed solution could be found. In that spirit, I refrained from taking any step which might have been construed as uncooperative or as jeopardizing the efforts then under way.

Imagine my dismay when, a couple of days ago, I discovered that during my absence on home leave the Executive Director, unknown to me, filed P.5 actions (copy attached) on 29 December 1989 intended to swap Mr. Vidal-Naquet's post with mine, and backdating everything to 28 July 1989. To keep me in the dark, even the letter sent to my office on 20 January 1990 after my return from leave, transmitting these P.5 actions to the Executive Office for verification and circulation, was addressed not to me, but to my deputy and successor-designate, Ms. Kate Starr-Newell, who quietly tucked it away. It was just by accident that I happened to spot a copy of the letter and P.5 action in my personal file almost a month afterwards. I do not know whether you yourself are aware of these particular P.5 actions. All I can say at the moment is that these dubious manoeuvres have spoiled the progress that I thought we had made and taken all of us back to square one.

My position is clear. I regard these P.5 actions as illegal, and I am requesting that they be rescinded, revoked or nullified. It is a shameless case of robbing Peter to give Paul, which, occurring in the United Nations, I find intolerable.

At this point, I would greatly appreciate it if you or the Executive Director would be kind enough to clarify for me five specific points:

1, Exactly why has the Executive Director decided to deprive me of a post which I have occupied since I joined the Council on 1 January 1984, the very post against which I was recruited and which I have encumbered from that day to this?

2. Exactly why has that post been awarded to Mr. Alain Vidal-Naquet?

3. Exactly why is the post hitherto encumbered by Mr. Alain Vidal-Naquet being assigned to me?

Whoever pretends that my post is being abolished is a liar because that post continues to exist on the WFC staffing table. If, on the other hand, the problem facing the Executive Director has been the managerial one of deciding whom to eliminate among the three D-1 staff, given that there are only two D-1 posts, then my fourth question is the real crux, and has to be answered to the satisfaction of all of us:

4. Exactly why has the Executive Director chosen to ignore the SecretaryGeneral's Administrative Instruction ST/AI/353 which spells out a clear-cut procedure to be followed by every Programme Manager, involving the use of Joint Departmental Advisory Panels, a procedure designed to exclude favouritism and ensure that all staff members are treated equally without discrimination or victimization? If there are only two D-1 positions in the Council, why should I, the most senior of the D-1s, not be given a chance to compete for them? Can a P.5 administrative action taken by an appointee of the Secretary-General such as the Executive Director, in flagrant violation of the Secretary-General's own Administrative Instruction (issued publicly to all members of the staff, and notified to all United Nations Permanent Missions) be regarded as legal?

5. Exactly why must the Executive Director's actions be so shrouded in secrecy? Of all things, a P.5 personnel action, once completed, is supposed to be furnished immediately to the staff member affected by such action. It is not to be handled as if it was a secret death warrant! Where is the transparency which

we talk of in the United Nations, an organization which the world regards as the custodian and arch-guardian of human rights?

Dear Mr. Annan, I submit to you that I am the victim of an illegal act, intentionally designed and perpetrated to kill my career, for no better reason than that I am standing in somebody's way. I am not just crying for a job and a salary. Something much higher is at stake – a cry for justice. I beseech you, as the highest official ultimately responsible to the Secretary-General for my welfare as a worker in this organization, to protect me. But if I must die, I will die in action, fighting. I will not lie down and close my eyes to be butchered.

Kindly favour me with an early reply as time has now become a significant factor. For your convenience, I am sending a copy of this letter directly to the Executive Director of the World Food Council. As soon as I have received your/his clarification to the above five points, I shall know whether to take my case to the Joint Appeals Board or, if I am so advised, directly to the Administrative Tribunal.

Thank you very much for your consideration.

Yours sincerely,

Peter E. Temu

Chief

World Food Council Liaison Office, New York".

Annex 2.

The Secretary-General's Administrative Instruction ST/AI/353.

The Executive Director's failure to observe the provisions of Administrative Instruction ST/AI/353 was one of his worst blunders. His decision to swap my "core" post with Mr. Vidal-Naquet's "non-core" post was not made in accordance with that administrative instruction. This rendered his action utterly indefensible. The instruction, dated 20 July 1988, reads as follows:

"UNITED NATIONS SECRETARIAT

Administrative Instruction ST/AI/353 dated 20 July 1988

To: Members of the staff

From: The Assistant Secretary-General for Human Resources Management

Subject: INTERNAL REASSIGNMENT OF STAFF: GUIDELINES FOR <u>AD HOC </u>JOINT DEPARTMENTAL ADVISORY PANELS

1. Revised estimates …have been submitted to the General Assembly as requested…Revised staffing tables will be issued shortly…

2. These staffing tables will serve as a basis for heads of departments and offices to complete their review of programme requirements and resource allocations and to plan for the necessary internal reassignment of their staff. In order to ensure that such staff reassignments are undertaken in a fair and objective manner, the Secretary-General has decided that ad hoc joint departmental advisory panels shall be established to advise heads of departments and offices on the internal reassignment of their staff.

3. These panels shall include between four and eight members, half of them to be nominated by the staff and the other half to be nominated by the head of department or office concerned. A representative of the Office of Human Resources Management or the local personnel office shall serve in an ex officio capacity. In the course of its work, a panel may decide to divide itself into two subgroups to deal separately with staff in the Professional and higher categories and staff in the General Service and related categories.

4. The functions of the departmental panels will be twofold:

   (a) To determine a preliminary list of staff members who should be reassigned when one or more posts among a group of similar posts at the same level have been slated for abolition;

   (b) To conduct a review of vacancies and projected vacancies up to 31 December 1989 in the department or office to determine whether the staff members on the departmental list determined under subparagraph (a), as well as those staff members who are encumbering specific posts already earmarked for abolition, could be reassigned within the department or office and to make appropriate recommendations to the head of the department or office.

5. In order for the panels to start their review, it will be necessary for them to have the results of the programmatic review of posts to be undertaken by the head of department or office. The programmatic review will distinguish between 'core posts' that will continue after 31 December 1989 and 'non-core posts' that will be abolished. It is therefore essential that the programmatic review be completed by the head of department or office concerned as soon as possible.

6. The department or office will provide the panel with a revised staffing table , and a list of staff, together with an up-to-date list of vacancies and projected vacancies up to 31 December 1989. At the same time, staff members who are on non-core posts identified for abolition or are on posts among a group of similar posts at the same level, some of which have been slated for abolition, shall be informed by the head of department or office concerned. All staff members under review shall be offered an opportunity to submit to the panel pertinent information relating to their case if they so wish.

7. In the discharge of its functions under paragraph 4(a) above, the panel shall take into account all relevant information, including input provided by chiefs of division, branch, service, section, etc. The four major criteria to be used in establishing the preliminary list of staff members to be reassigned shall be their official record of performance, their integrity, the length of their service in the Organization and their qualifications for the post they encumbered. In the course of its review, the

panel shall also have due regard for equitable geographical balance and gender.

8. Once the panel has established a preliminary list of staff members to be reassigned, the panel shall then undertake a review of all staff members on that list, together with those who are encumbering posts specifically earmarked for abolition on programmatic grounds, with a view to matching the staff members concerned with all existing and projected vacancies at their respective levels in the department or office up to 31 December 1989 in accordance with paragraph 4(b) above. In the course of that review, the panel may also take into account those staff members considered under paragraph 4 (a) above who have not been placed on the preliminary list.

9. In the discharge of its functions under paragraph 4(b) above, the panel shall give priority to the staff members under review for lateral reassignment to any current or projected vacancy in accordance with the following criteria. The broad requirements of the post must be met. For this purpose, a candidate who has the relevant education, as well as sufficient and satisfactory experience in the main area of work covered by the vacant post, shall be deemed qualified. Other critical criteria shall be the contractual status of the candidates, their record of performance, their integrity and the length of their service with the Organization, In the course of its review, the panel shall also have due regard for equitable geographical balance and gender.

10. Upon completion of this one-time ad hoc review, the panel shall conclude its work by presenting to the head of department or office a list of staff members to be placed against existing or

projected vacant posts within the department or office for his or her approval. Should the head of department or office not be able fully to endorse the list, he or she shall advise the panel in writing and shall request the panel to undertake a further review in the light of the written explanations provided. If differences remain, the panel may bring them to the attention of the Assistant Secretary-General for Human Resources Management, in the context of the vacancy management exercise."

ANNEX 3.

THE EXECUTIVE DIRECTOR TURNS DOWN UNDP's REQUEST FOR MY SERVICES.

Five letters were exchanged between UNDP New York and WFC Rome in the course of one week: 11 -18 October 1991. This goes to show the urgency of the matter, as a reading of the letters clearly indicates. At issue was UNDP's request for my services for three weeks immediately preceding my return to Rome, a request which the Executive Director flatly refused - thereby undermining, willingly or by default, UNDP/WFC cooperation permanently. Three of the letters are reproduced below.

3.1 Letter dated 14 October 1991 from Mr. Trant to me,

"Dear Peter,

Thank you for your note of 10 October 1991, in reply to mine to you, concerningyour imminent return to Rome.

I have just now received the attached letter from Mr. Basem Khader, Officer-in-Charge, Regional Bureau for Africa in UNDP, requesting your services for three weeks starting 17 October 1991. I understand that you have indicated to Mr. Khader your willingness to undertake this assignment, which would involve travel to ESAMI in Tanzania.

I would appreciate hearing from you on the following points: 1) Do you indeed agree to UNDP's proposal? and: 2) if so, how do you intend to fulfil the three week assignment and still report to duty in Rome on 1 November?

I would also be interested in knowing if you really do have "no other pressing engagements at the moment", as reported in Mr. Khader's letter. As Principal Officer of the World Food Council in New York and soon-to-be Chief of an important unit in the secretariat in Rome, it surprises me that you are not fully occupied by the current General Assembly session and/or with preparations for your forthcoming duties here.

In view of Mr, Khader's request for a prompt response, I look forward to your reply to me at your earliest opportunity.

Yours sincerely

Gerald I. Trant

Executive Director"

3.2 Letter dared 16 October 1991 from me to Mr. Trant in reply to his of 14 October 1991.

"Dear Gerry,

Thank you for your letter of 14 October 1991 concerning UNDP's request for my services. I am responding promptly as requested to avoid further delay.

The duties of the post I will fill in Rome have always included, among other things, attendance at GA sessions in Geneva and New York, and follow-up on the UNDP/WFC TCDC umbrella project entitled South-South cooperation in the food and agriculture sector, one component of which is the ESAMI food security analysis and management training project, which is the subject of this correspondence.

As we both know, the last incumbent of that post, Mr. Alain Vidal-Naquet, covered both the GA sessions and this TCDC project consistently, right up to the time of his retirement in September 1990. Indeed, in the case of the TCDC project, he continued to cover it for a time even after his retirement. As his successor, I see my participation in GA sessions and in the TCDC project as following naturally in his footsteps and I view both as part of my preparation to assume my new duties in Rome.

Despite my new duties, announced by you after the current GA session had opened, you have not up to this writing designated me, as your Principal Officer in New York and soon-to-be Chief of that important secretariat unit in Rome, to represent you in the General Assembly proceedings in any capacity. Instead, you have officially designated two other senior officers to cover the session. These are Ms. Kate Newell, who is Officer-in-Charge of the Liaison Office, and Ms. Anne Rogers, whom you are sending from Rome to New York to represent the Council at the GA session from 21 October to 1 November. In these circumstances, the surprise you express at my not being "fully occupied by the current General Assembly session" leaves me utterly perplexed!

In these circumstances too, I simply could not, in all sincerity, when approached by the UNDP, have claimed that I had pressing official engagements which prevented me from acceding to their request. In truth, the only pressing task I have on hand just now is a private one – namely, moving house and family to Rome at short notice. But where duty calls, I always put my family needs last and the needs of the service first. That is exactly what I have done. Knowing that the UNDP/WFC TCDC project on South-South co-operation in the food and agriculture sector, in which I actively participated last April, has now become an inherent part of the responsibilities which I am about to assume in Rome, I saw it as my duty to co-operate fully with UNDP. I felt certain I could be faulted if I did not. I am frankly dismayed by the irony that my decision to co-operate is now being questioned.

You rightly raise the question whether it is possible to do the assignment and still report to Rome in time. Originally, this would have been perfectly possible. But given the delay that has already occurred, and may yet occur, some flexibility will be necessary if I am to proceed with the assignment. Either I report to Rome a little later, or the duration of the assignment is made a little shorter, or both. But these are points of detail which I could thrash out with my colleagues at the UNDP once your clearance has been obtained, and always subject to your final approval.

Before I end, perhaps I should dispel one possible misconception. The UNDP assignment involves much more than just a trip to ESAMI. The UNDP wants me to travel to Harare, Zimbabwe, the seat of SADCC's eastern and southern Africa's food security programme to meet its director, Professor Mandivana Rukuni; to the UNISR in Geneva to meet its director, Professor Dharam Ghai; and to Oxford, England, to meet Dr. Roger Hay, who is Director of the Food Studies Group. Apparently, it is UNDP's intention to involve all these institutions, in addition to ESAMI, in this TCDC project.

The mission is therefore important. The UNDP has informed me that its launching of the major project on schedule in early 1992 depends on the success and timeliness of my mission , and the quality of the <u>project document</u> which is expected to emanate from it. I am flattered by UNDP's faith in my ability to discharge the task as is evident in their letter to you. This is good for WFC's image. Personally, I see no reason to disappoint them, particularly at this late hour when arrangements are so far advanced (see their internal memo to show how far they are already preparing in anticipation of your positive reply).

Nevertheless, I have made it crystal-clear that I will only go along with the request if I have your unreserved support. The decision is yours. I have no personal interest in the matter, beyond a plea that the decision be made quickly, one way or the other. Whichever way it is, I shall dutifully oblige, and get on with the job. But if the intention is that I take up the assignment then it is clear that I have to start right away.

With kind regards,
Yours sincerely,

Peter E. Temu
Principal Officer"

3.3 Letter dated 18 October 1991
from Trant to myself in reply to mine of 16 October 1991.

"Dear Peter,

I acknowledge receipt of your letter of 16 October 1991 regarding your proposed mission for UNDP.

As I recall, the project on South-South co-operation in the food and agricultural sector consists of three elements: an interregional consultation, a food industry component and a training component. The interregional consultation was held under the auspices of the WFC (Cairo April 1991) and the implementation of the food industry component was entrusted to UNIDO. As for the remaining component, I declined UNDP's request that WFC become directly involved in it, since, as you know, WFC does not engage in training and other operational activities.

In view of this, but more importantly, because I consider the duties awaiting you in Rome more important to WFC's activities, I am unable to agree to the proposal that you be lent to UNDP in order to prepare training materials under the South-South project. I remain nevertheless committed to collaborating further with UNDP in following up on this project in the area of policy development, at a time which is mutually convenient for WFC and UNDP. I shall be informing Mr. Khader accordingly.

In your letter of 16 October you indicate, based on an internal UNDP memorandum dated 14 October, that your mission with UNDP involves visiting Arusha, Harare, Geneva, Oxford and subsequently returning to New York to formulate a draft project document. It is doubtful that you could achieve this before reporting for duty to WFC in Rome on 1 November 1991.

The suggestion, contained in you letter of 16 October, that if you are unable to report to WFC on 1 November, it will be because of unspecified delays in the approval of your mission, presumably at this end, is frankly unacceptable. The letter from UNDP requesting that you be released by WFC beginning 17 October is dated Friday,11 October and reached me Monday, 14 October. I replied on the same day. In any case, no organization can seriously be requested to release one of its officers on 3 days notice.

As for the South-South project being the responsibility of the chief of the external relations unit, I should point out that Mr. Vidal-Naquet was assigned the responsibility of looking after it because he had contributed to its formulation and approval, largely through personal contacts. Since WFC is interested in the policy development component of this project, after Mr. Vidal-Naquet's departure from WFC, I assigned the responsibility for the monitoring and follow-up to Mr. Uwe Kracht, Chief, Policy Development and Economic Analysis.

I would like you to report to Rome without further delay. If you can make yourself available before 1 November 1991, all the better.

Yours sincerely,

Gerald I. Trant
Executive Director"

Annex 4.

The Executive Director's qualified 'welcome' to me to return to Rome.

In his reluctance to have me back in Rome, the Executive Director stated in his invitation letter that I was not a "perfect match" for the post. I took him to task for openly expressing such a prejudice.

1.1 Letter dated 20 September 1991
from Mr. Trant to me

"Dear Peter,

Please see my memo to Mr. Ciss. Welcome back to Rome.

Best regards,
Yours sincerely,
Gerry   Trant
Executive Director"

4.2 Letter dated 10 October from me to Mr. Trant in reply to his dated 20 September 1991.

"Dear Gerry,

I acknowledge with thanks receipt of your letter dated 20 September 1991 inviting me to take up new responsibilities in Rome as Chief, Policy Co-ordination and External Relations.

I welcome an opportunity when we can all put the past behind us, and pull together in the interests of the Council. Till we meet, I remain,

Yours sincerely,
Peter E. Temu"

4.3 Letter dated 20 September 1991 from Mr. Trant to Mr. Abdou Ciss

"To: Mr. Abdou Ciss
Assistant Secretary-General
Human Resources Management

From: Gerald I. Trant
Executive Director
World Food Council

Subject: Mr Peter Temu

This memorandum accompanies the P5 action form for Mr. Temu which responds to Mr. Foran's memoranda of 2 August 1991 and 17 September 1991.

Mr. Temu will be placed against the important post of Head of External Relations and Council Affairs, a D1 level post. While the post and the proposed incumbent are not a perfect match, it is essential that this important post be filled as soon as possible. It would be impractical to change the functions of the post simply to suit an individual without regard to the needs of the World Food Council.

The position is here in Rome and there is a great deal of work to de done. Consequently the 1 November 1991 starting date is the latest time by which the post should be filled".

4.4 Letter dated 26 September 1991 from Ms. King to me

"To: Mr. Peter Temu
Principal Officer, World Food Council, NYO

From: Angela E.V. King, Director
Staff Administration and Training Division, OHRM

Subject: Reassignment to Rome

As confirmed to you by telephone on 23 September, I am pleased to inform you that Mr. Trant has agreed to reassign you to Rome with a D-1 level post as Head of External Relations and Council Affairs.

I understand from Mr. Comba that you would be expected to take up your duties on 1 November 1991. I trust that now that the matter of your assignment has been resolved you will make every effort to relocate by 1 November.

I wish you every success in this assignment and you can count on the full support of OHRM and of your Personnel Officer, Mr. Vadim Padalka, in facilitating your move.

I attach the relevant P.5 action

4.5 Letter from me to Ms. King
in reply to hers of 26 September 1991

"To: Ms. Angela E. V. King, Director
Staff Administration and Training Division
Office of Human Resources Management

From: Peter E. Temu, Principal Economic Affairs Officer
World Food Council Office in New York

Subject: My reassignment to Rome

Thank you for your memo dated 26 September 1991, enclosing a copy of the P.5 action for my transfer to Rome. I have also received from Mr. Gerald Trant a copy of his memorandum of 20 September 1991 addressed to Mr. Abdou Ciss and copied to Mr. Richard Foran, among others.

In that memorandum, Mr. Trant refers to two memoranda from Mr. Foran dated 2 August and 17 September 1991. The same reference has been made on the P.5 action which you sent me. Since this exchange of correspondence, along with the P.5 action, would appear to constitute the terms of my transfer, I request that I be given copies of the same for my information and records.

I notice that in spite of his own decision to assign me to an important post in Rome, Mr. Trant states that he does not consider me a "perfect match" for the post, and that he would not change the functions of a post "simply to suit an individual". These remarks bother me. Whether or not this was their intention, such remarks have three unfortunate effects on me. The first is the intimidation I feel, that I either perform or else! The second is my feeling that Mr. Trant is prejudging my performance even before I assume my new functions. It is as if Mr. Trant is preparing the ground for the day when he can make a formal "evaluation", decide that my performance is bad, and simply say to Mr. Ciss and Mr. Foran, "I told you so".

The third is the bad effect on morale his announcement is bound to have, on the part of my colleagues generally, but more especially on those who will be working under my supervision after being told by the Executive Director that I, their supervisor, fall short of the demands of my responsibilities.

I am most reluctant and a bit embarrassed to be saying this, but I am sure you will understand why I have had to do so for the record. For, apart from the fact that few people can claim to be a perfect match for the posts they hold, it is a rare departure from normal practice for a Chief Executive to extend this kind of "welcome" to his immediate subordinate on the eve of assigning him important new responsibilities.

This having been said, I must make it absolutely clear to you, to my colleagues in the Council and to the Executive Director, that I am looking forward whole-heartedly to my return to Rome where I can continue, as in the past, to work shoulder to shoulder, loyally and effectively, with everyone else in the Council in pursuit of our common objective.

Before I end, may I express my sincere gratitude to you personally, to your colleagues in OHRM and to many others at the United Nations Headquarters who have handled my case with fairness and firmness through two very difficult years. It is reassuring for me to know that, as we close this unhappy chapter, I can continue to count on your full support."

Annex 5.

Official Record of the author's Performance Evaluation Reports: 1977-1986.

What appears below is a summary of my Performance Evaluation Reports from the time I was recruited in ECA in 1977, to the time of my job crisis with WFC in 1989. This is the official record as maintained in the files of the Office of Personnel at United Nations Headquarters in New York. The ratings for 1986 to 1989 were never filed, because they were biased, rebutted by the author, and discarded by the U.N.

Period	Office and Duty Station	Final Rating (on a scale of 1 to 6)	Name of Supervisor 1st/2nd Reporting Officer
		Rating	Comment
1977 -1979	ECA Addis Ababa	2 A very good performance	Nomvete/Adedeji
1981-1981	ECA Addis Ababa	1 An outstanding performance	Nomvete/Adedeji

1981-1982	ECA Addis Ababa	1 An outstanding performance	Nomvete/Adedeji
1983	ECA Addis Ababa	1 An outstanding performance	Bazin/Adedeji
1984	WFC Rome	1 An excellent performance	Williams/Williams
1985-1986	WFC Rome	1 An excellent performance	Trant/Trant
1986-1989	WFC New York	Biased: Rebutted, and Discarded.	Trant/Trant

---

Annex 6:

The seniority ladder and official designations of United Nations professional staff

This is for the information of those who may not be familiar with the United Nations seniority levels, designations, and the corresponding salary scales of the professional staff. Holders of the SG, USG, and ASG level posts are usually political appointees; whereas all professional posts from P-1 to D-2 are promotional, and their staff recruitment and promotion is the responsibility of the U.N. Appointments and Promotions Board. The designations given below are the official seniority titles: actual titles or designations at the duty station may differ (e.g. Director-General, Executive Secretary, Executive Director, Administrator, High Commissioner, Resident Representative, Chief, Director, etc.) depending on the organization's constitutional structure and the nature of the incumbent's responsibilities.

SG	Secretary-General	P-5	Senior Officer
USG	Under-Secretary-General	P-4	Senior Officer
ASG	Assistant Secretary-General	P-3	Officer
D-2	Director	P-2	Junior Officer
D-1	Principal Officer	P-1	Junior Officer

www.ingramcontent.com/pod-product-compliance
Lightning Source LLC
Chambersburg PA
CBHW061407280526
45784CB00001B/395